It Came, To

IT CAME, TO PASS

An Autobiography

৵৽৽

Margaret D. Jones

APECS Press
Caerleon

First published in 2007 by APECS Press

Editing, design and typesetting by
APECS Press Caerleon

The publisher acknowledges the financial support
of the Welsh Books Council

ISBN 978-0-9548940-2-3

Printed in Wales by
Dinefwr Press, Llandybïe, Carmarthenshire

To Basil and our family

Preface

IT was my good fortune, in the twenty-five years from 1980, to illustrate for publication a number of the great traditional tales of the world, especially the stories of my adoptive country of Wales. Now I am urged to write an account of how that came to pass. I like that biblical phrase, "came to pass". In three small words it describes the whole process of life. Events come, in order to pass, and are followed by others, which in turn fall behind the next, as Time goes on its inexorable way. Everything comes—and passes.

I have had a generous slice of life's cake, and I have eaten every crumb with relish. Soon it will all be gone, and the plate will be empty. Yet, undeniably, it did all happen, and none of it can be altered or wiped out now. Any part of the past is as real as the present, which tomorrow will have joined. It would be nice to think, that somehow, somewhere, man's genius will one day find a way of tapping into such a record and re-living it all over again; or, to revert to my first metaphor, a way in which we can have our cake and eat it. I wouldn't bank on it! Indeed, I think such a marvel is as much of a fairy-tale as any I have pictured for children's books. So I will do as I have been urged to do, and make my meagre record here.

Looking back, I realise that I can recall only a tiny fraction of the whole. We forget so much more than we remember; and it is not always the significant milestones that stick in our minds and leave their mark, but unexpected snippets and trivialities. Memories are like the tide going out on a beach, leaving behind little pools and puddles in which we may fish for souvenirs of our holidays. This narrative will be just a bucketful of assorted flotsam.

To anyone looking for thrills and adventures, or a tale of derring-do, played out against brave odds, I must warn that you will be disappointed. My life is notable only for its outstanding normality. I have had no traumatic experiences, no awful accident or un-deserved sorrow, no relative with an incurable medical condition, no unexpected bereavement—not even any tangled relationship or interesting sexual diversion! Nor can I claim to have been on intimate terms with any of today's superstars. I did once shake hands with Pandit Nehru, and met his daughter Indira Ghandi; but it was brief, and I am sure they would not have remembered it. I can think of no-one else in that league. So perhaps you could say that my story has "rarity attraction" and makes a welcome change of reading. That is my hope anyway.

Contents

Part One

BEGINNINGS

BEGINNINGS

✺

One

Norths and Atkinsons

WHEN, on occasion I have had to fill in a form on which there is space left for place of birth, I have written, Bromley, Kent. But I do not know the town, which has no doubt changed a great deal since I first drew breath in it. I have never been back there since. The event was on the twenty-eighth day of December 1918. My mother came from south-east England and already had one child, a boy, my brother Chris, who was fifteen months old. My father was not present. I do not mean only that he was not present at the birth, which would have been an unusual concession in those days to say the least. He was out of the country at the time.

Christopher North was a minister of the Methodist Church, with degrees and a special interest in Old Testament studies. He had offered his services for missionary work, and was stationed in the

Benares district of India. He served there for only a short while, before he was obliged to return to Britain, since my mother, who was never very robust, was pronounced by her doctors to be not strong enough for life in a tropical climate. It must have been a severe blow for his hopes and plans. At the time of my birth, Mother was attended by her older sister, my aunt Gertrude Atkinson.

My father's origins were in Lancashire, where he had been brought up under the shadow of Pendle Hill, in the village of Downham, near Clitheroe. He was the eldest of four children, three boys and a girl, and he was only twelve when their father, Richard North, an accountant, died. The two elder boys, Christopher and Harold, were sent to an orphanage school—I do not know where that was. He had almost nightmare memories of the place—the bullying and indignities—and they seemed to dominate his mind when he was dying at the age of 87. He and Harold felt it to be a great stigma being sent to such a school, but they were both extremely bright boys. I later possessed a number of books with beautiful real leather covers, embossed in gold with the orphanage crest, and with gold-edged pages, which had been awarded as prizes to the brothers for their prowess in various subjects. One was a large, magnificent, illustrated volume of the complete works of Shakespeare, presented to Harold North, "for good behaviour, by the vote of the whole school"! To my infinite regret, it was lost (or pinched) when we had to move house during the Second World War and leave some of our books in storage.

Dad was an ambitious young man, and gained his objectives and made his career by sheer determination. He used to tell me proudly that he had had to teach himself Latin in order to gain a college entrance.

I know little of my antecedents, but a distant cousin, drawing on the reminiscences of my father's youngest aunt, gathered some facts and passed them on. I understand that one of the Norths was born, as they say, "on the wrong side of the blanket", and we owed our name to his mother, who was never married. There was a Victorian pawnbroker somewhere amongst them too, though his two daughters complained that he was never in the shop but left them to run it while he idled away his time. So, if I were to design my own coat-of-arms, perhaps I should include three balls somewhere in a corner.

My father's mother, Grandma North, I remember as a stern, uncompromising woman. No doubt she had known hard times, bringing up four children on her own, with little means after her husband died; but on the few occasions when she visited our household, we children were afraid of her. She was strict and censorious and rarely smiled. In my memory, she always wears a black hat and looks out from under it with a disapproving expression.

In contrast, Grandma Atkinson, on my mother's side, was always smiling as if life was a music-hall joke. She wore a large, heavily-decorated hat and, when I knew her, was usually dressed in black down to her ankles—almost obligatory for an elderly widow in those days. She always wore a delicate collar of white net, separate from the dress and covered by its neckline. It stood up against her neck, with a frilly lace edging under her chin, and was kept upright with thin slats of whalebone. It was changed and washed every day.

Grandpa Atkinson died when I was about one or two years old and I do not remember him. He was a fishmonger, but a grander one than that implies, for he owned several shops and other people did the work in them. We are talking "upper middle-class" here. The Atkinsons always gave a set of silver fish knives and forks as wedding presents, and when I married, a similar gift was presented to me; I still have the remnants of it. So, another corner of that coat-of-arms that I am contemplating should definitely include a crossed fish-knife and fork.

They were a large family, the Atkinsons. I believe that Grandma Atkinson had eleven or twelve children, but a number of them died in infancy. My mother's name was Dolly, short for Dorothy May. Her brothers and sisters bore names equally redolent of those times; besides Dolly and Gertrude, there were Nellie, Aubrey, Lesley, Bertha, Clarise, Elsie and Kitty. Nellie, the eldest, always spoken of

Formal group at my parents' wedding in Bromley, Kent, 1916.

with affection, was a "hunchback" they said, and died before I was born. It was confidently asserted that I "took after her", not because of her poor health—mine was always of the rudest sort—but as a budding artist. How that could be I did not try to work out. There were a number of small, but heavily-framed oil paintings by her, mainly of cows in shady meadows, hanging in Grandma's drawing room.

My mother was very pretty, with large brown eyes and a mass of dark hair piled on top of her head. But she was a timid soul, and suffered frequently with migraines and 'nerves'. My father was tall, blue-eyed and handsome, and always very much the master in his own household. I have the big photograph of their wedding and they make an undoubtedly good-looking couple. It was 1916, during the Great War, and a number of the male guests are in military uniform. There are the parents, and the bridesmaids in their enormous decorated hats, in the front row—Gertrude and Bertha and Clarise and Elsie, and my father's sister, also called Gertrude. It all looks a very much grander affair than my own wedding, twenty-six years later, when Britain was again suffering under the strictures of war.

After my father died, many years later, my brother Chris told me that Dad had confided in him one day that he had never really wanted the marriage, but he had been "tricked into it". As children, we were never subjected to open quarrels between our parents; but children are much more astute than grown-ups give them credit for. Even at a young age, we sensed uncomfortably if Mother was unhappy or Dad irritated by her meekness and lack of self-assertion; for I am sure that was what it mainly was. The Atkinsons were staunch Methodists, prominent pillars of the local chapel, and an up-and-coming young minister of the denomination would be a real catch. Perhaps he was entertained in their house as the visiting preacher on a Sunday, and perhaps he was a little over-attentive to this pretty, delicate daughter who was too modest to push for herself. Then perhaps, her over-eager family jumped in and treated the matter as a *fait accompli*, and he was trapped. I am largely guessing;

but in that big photograph amongst all those smiling faces, the bride-groom does not look a happy man.

I sensed that my mother was something of a pet among her more self-confident sisters and at times they tut-tutted and hinted that my father was not as kind to her as he might have been. He was strong and ambitious and clever, and though he did his best when she was ill, it must have been frustrating for him. She was not without skills of her own, especially in the art of needlework and embroidery, lace and dress-making. I still have an exquisite linen tablecloth which she made before she was married; she embroidered and edged it with hand-crocheted lace, four to five inches wide all round. But she found running a house, and especially coping with maidservants, at times beyond her powers.

Later, after Barbara and Bronwen were born, we were quite often sent to Grandma Atkinson's house during school holidays. I suspect Mother found it hard to cope with us all, especially my over-assertive self—and I was the most frequent choice for these visits. I loved going, so it posed no problem. Grandma lived with her three unmarried daughters in a pleasant house in Heathdene Road, Wallington, Surrey, not far from Croydon, and within easy reach by train of London. The three aunts were Gertrude, Bertha and Clarise.

Aunt Gert, who had been with Mother when I was born and Dad was abroad in India, took me under her wing, and it seemed to be generally agreed that I was her particular charge. She, like my mother, was very pretty, judging by photographs, but she had suffered two bitter disappointments in love. The first young man had walked out most shamefully—I know nothing more of the circumstances than that. The second, a soldier named Frank, she had met while work-ing as a Red Cross auxiliary nurse during the Great War. She had really loved him and she had a fine diamond engagement ring that he had given her and which came to me years later after she died. But Frank had been killed at the Front and Gertrude was, like hundreds of other young women of her generation, bereft of love and a happy future by that terrible event in history, at a time when the label "old maid" still bore an unfair and undeserved stigma. She never did marry, and she patently wished that I could have been the child she would never have.

After Nellie died, Gertrude was the eldest of the sisters, the next being Bertha, loyal Methodist and Grandma's right hand. On the not-infrequent occasions that I went to stay with them, I usually slept in Gertrude's room, or even, when I was small, in her bed. Grandma and Bertha had twin beds in the big bedroom. As time went on, Gertrude grew more bitter and discontented, and would mutter her rebellious thoughts to me, trying to get me "on her side", and make it "Them and Us".

Grandma and Bertha would take me to the Ladies' Sewing Guild at the Methodist church. There I sat among the grown-ups, and was given balls of wool, to make a piece of French knitting. Four little nails were tacked into the top of a wooden cotton-reel (they are all made of plastic now, and can't be so used); and the art was to twine the thread into a tube of knitting, which hung through the hole in the reel, and which could afterwards be stitched into coils, making mats or other "useful" articles.

Gertrude, on the other hand, had joined the Anglican Church in nearby Carshalton. It was a particularly "high-church" establishment, and the vicar was reputed to have definite Roman leanings. I never quite worked out whether Gert made her choice from genuine similar inclinations, or as a defiant gesture of rebellion against the Methodist tide and the holy alliance between her mother and her sister. In her later years she went the whole way and joined the Roman Catholic Church; I believe she found it a comfort to her lonely, disappointed soul. When I grew to an age in which I could be allowed to make some of my own choices, Gertrude asked me if I would like to go to an Anglican service with her, one Sunday morning. It seemed like an interesting adventure to me, and one well worth trying out, so I agreed. While Grandma and Bertha, hatted and decently gloved, and in shoes that shone like liquorice, set out for chapel, Gert and I caught the bus to Carshalton. "I don't know what your father would say!" Bertha declared, with disapproval in every line of her face and posture. But that only added relish to my anti-establishment adventure, and Gert and I were bonded as fellow-rebels.

My father would not have objected at all. He had been a member of the Anglican community himself, before switching to the Methodists. I found the atmosphere of theatre, the robes and litany, the sprayed incense, and the great crucifix bearing its suffering figure, exciting, at that age, but I never shared Gertrude's wish to sever myself from the familiar ethos of chapel. That was where birth had landed me and I belonged there. A self-assertive child I may have been but I was not a true rebel. I sensed that, when I was staying with them, Gert made the most of a potential ally, and widened the gap; but if her conspiratorial whispers grew too outrageous, I would exclaim: "Oh Auntie! It's not really like that!" and she would subside into silence.

The third unmarried aunt was Clarise, who, like Grandma, always had a twinkle in her eye. She was more independent than the other two, in that she had an office job of some kind in Wallington, and went out to work each day. Gertrude, letting family secrets out of the bag, to her favourite niece, told me one day that Clarise had once, when very young, become attached to a young man and had actually borne his child—out of wedlock! Apparently there was no question of a marriage; perhaps he was already married, or perhaps he, too, had died in the fighting. How I wish I had been more curious in those days, and pumped them all with questions. But the young are always too wrapped up in their own concerns, and too inclined to dismiss the past in favour of the future. Bertha would probably have refused to tell me more on this occasion, and Gert would certainly have got into trouble for telling me anything at all.

Grandma and Bertha, it seemed, had hushed up the whole affair. Clarise was whisked away for a "holiday", and the child was immediately sent for adoption. I believe it was a boy.

The house in Heathdene Road was sizeable. I can see now in my mind's eye, the dining room, with its large grandfather clock which chimed self-importantly every hour; and a big mahogany sideboard, which bore at either end heavy matching bronzes, each of a muscular man wrestling with a spirited horse. Grandma sat in her leather armchair all day, like a queen on her throne, and twinkled at us over her pinz-nez.

There was an attic, too, and in a room at the top of a between-walls staircase, was a big trunk, full of discarded clothing. There were the usual beflowered hats, feather boas, fans and scarves. We children adored dressing-up, and even putting on "shows" for an appreciative audience. I always loved anything to do with drama and costume and lights. Aunt Gert was generous in taking me on trips to the theatres in London, and I remember vividly going to the Old Vic with her, on more than one occasion. We saw "Lilac-Time" and Wagner's "Lohengrin", and others. The more romantic it was, the better Aunt Gert liked it.

I remember another occasion, when Aunt Bertha had tickets for us all to go and see a performance by the Amateur Dramatic Society of the Methodist church. I had been looking forward all day to the evening with mounting excitement. I didn't care if it was amateur or an all-star cast; it was colour and story and atmosphere. But when Bertha came to go through the modest contents of my suitcase, she decided there was nothing in it fit to wear for such an occasion. My poor mother had to dress three of us (I had a younger sister by then) and no doubt did not find it easy on a Methodist minister's salary. Despite my despairing howls, and despite Gertrude's pleas on my behalf, I was told that it was out of the question. I could not go to the performance in the Methodist Hall dressed in any of the clothes I had brought with me from home; they simply were not respectable enough. So I stayed at home with a sympathetic Gertrude while the rest went, and I still recall my sobbing, searing disappointment.

Clarise sometimes took us to the cinema in Wallington, in those early days when Talkies were an innovation. I remember going with her to see Jessie Matthews in "Daddy Longlegs", a romantic film with a piano accompaniment. My brother was there too, and we both much preferred the supporting film, which had an entire cast of chimpanzees, dressed up like humans and twice as entertaining. We talked of little else for days afterwards, and laughed ourselves nearly sick over it.

There was never any shortage of money in the house in Wallington. Grandpa Atkinson's fish shops had left them all pretty well-off. They bought a holiday bungalow in Tankerton, near Whitstable on the Kent coast, and sometimes we went to spend a seaside holiday with them there. They framed some of my childish paintings and hung them round the walls. There was a wooden beach chalet which they rented. We could spend whole days by the sea, changing our clothes and even cooking and eating meals in the chalet. It was an exotic holiday with a comfortable sense of belonging thrown in, something you don't experience in a hotel in an alien land. They were pleasant days indeed.

Grandma died during the Second World War, and after I married, my lines were cast in different places, far from south-east England. I saw little of the aunts, even Aunt Gertrude, who died in her early seventies. Aunt Bertha did get married to a widower, later in life. I will not demean Aunt Gert by saying she was jealous, but it undoubtedly added to her feeling that Fate had been niggardly towards herself. I hope I did not contribute too much to her disappointment, but life went on and brought me interests and involvements of my own.

Two

❧

Early Days

AFTER my father returned from India, he was posted to a church in Shoreham, Kent, where my sister Barbara was born, two and a half years younger than I was. It was the policy of the Methodist church in those days to move their ministers every three years or so. It must have made things difficult for families with young children, settling into schools; but we were too young then to be affected. The next move was to Egham in Surrey, on the River Thames. My memories of both periods are few and hazy, and I am never quite sure in which home they occurred. I can see a dining-room window on a winter's morning, with a magical row of long, glassy icicles hanging from the frame.

I was the proud possessor of a small doll's pram, which I pushed around the garden, and I remember a little friend, older than I, who turned up to play one day with a larger pram, filled with an assortment of dolls and soft toys. Weirdly, she had tied handkerchiefs over all their faces, obscuring them. "Because", she said, "they all turned into goblins during the night, and they are too ugly to look at". I was struck with a fearful but delighted sense of awe, and never questioned the truth of her assertion.

I remember an evening when I had been given a balloon, which seemed very special because its colour was silver. Someone performed the dangerous operation of connecting it to the pipe of the kitchen stove, and filling it with gas, before tying it up. Then it was given to me to hold while we went into the darkening garden and looked up at the round, silver moon above us in the sky.

"Let it go!" I was urged. "It's a little moon, and it will fly all the way up to its mother". So though I was loth to lose my beautiful balloon, I raised my arm and let it go free. I can still see it floating up, magically lit by the dying daylight, on and on, higher and higher, until we could no longer see it. And I still wonder if it ever reached the moon. Childhood memories are made of such things.

I was a self-willed child. My father called it 'headstrong', and my playmates no doubt said, 'Bossy'. I have a photograph that shows me, at the age of about four, standing self-confidently on a large stone by the River Thames, a favourite spot for picnics. I have a face as round as a full moon, dark, straight hair cut in a bob with a fringe, and crowned with an enormous ribbon bow; and legs like young tree trunks. My father, who never pulled his punches, described them as, 'a good pair of understandings', and added: "Well, Peggy, you'll never be had up for having no visible means of support!" 'Peggy' was the diminutive of Margaret by which I was known from the start.

When I was about six, my father was appointed Hebrew and Old Testament lecturer at the Methodist training college in Handsworth Wood, Birmingham, and we moved there, to remain until the war in 1940. The house we were to live in was large and beautiful, and called 'Tranby'. In recent years my sister went there and asked to be allowed to see the old home. It had been made into flats, and one occupant asked her, "Do you mean to say that just one family lived in all this space?"

The rooms were large and spacious. It had a big cellar—never in our Methodist household used for strong wines. On the ground floor were kitchen and scullery and larder, dining room, lounge, and study for my father. There were four bedrooms on the first floor and a bathroom. The top floor consisted of two rooms and one which was just a space under the rafters, with no proper floor or ceiling, but with a narrow, unglazed window. I once opened the door to it, with some trepidation, to peer inside, and there was a large white barn owl sitting on the beam. The birds had nested there for years, coming and going through the window-slit, and they were regarded as the guardians of our home, like the ravens in the Tower of London.

The house had a sizeable garden, with a wide lawn, herbaceous borders full of lupins in summer, and a very large pear-tree that provided a good crop of fruit every year. Beyond that was a vegetable patch, and around it stretched the college grounds, playing fields, tennis courts, a squash court, and a wide drive up to the main entrance, with thick shrubberies on either side.

We children were free to roam over it all; and we climbed the trees, made secret dens in the shrubberies, and sat in Summer in the long grass which edged the field, almost hidden by the buttercups. There was a wall around it all, and a gate at the back which was locked and could not be entered from outside without a key. We considered ourselves apart from the children who lived in the terraced houses edging the street outside. Sometimes we would open the gate just a little, and peer out daringly. If there were any of them about there might be an exchange of rude words from both sides. We, of course, always felt safe in the knowledge that we could slam the gate and run away if things got too hot.

There were three gardeners who tended all the grounds, including a big vegetable plot which supplied the college kitchen. Chief of them was Mr Beddoes, who lived in the lodge at the main gates with Mrs Beddoes and George their son, also a gardener. With Mr Hickman, they kept our patch tidy every Friday. I think our vegetables were more in danger from us than from marauding birds. We used to raid the line of peas, well hidden by the tall sticks which supported them and eat our fill, enjoying forbidden fruit.

My Father developed a liking for gardening too, partly I think to keep his figure trim. He cut down much rampant growth, and planted shrubs like azaleas and rhododendron. We played French cricket on the lawn, and swung in the hammock under the apple trees. Next door, the New Testament lecturer, Dr Howard lived in an exactly similar house with his family, and we played with the two daughters, Joan and Margaret and Stephen their younger brother.

I can remember the evening when Mr Beddoes came to erect a revolving summerhouse for us, at the end of the lawn. We children had been bedded down and wished 'Goodnight', but it was still daylight for some hours, and I made an excuse to pay an exceedingly long visit to the toilet from which, with the window pushed up a couple of inches, I could watch the whole procedure. It would turn round on little wheels so that one could face the sun or block out the wind; but we were strictly forbidden to use it as a carousel, which we were quite prepared to do, spinning it round as fast as we could, with one of us inside enjoying the ride.

Chris attended a preparatory school for boys, and Barbara and I walked there and back every day to Miss Lowe's Primary school, 'The Laurels', about a mile away. This was before the days of many cars when roads were safe for small children to walk alone. I have few lasting memories of the place, but one stands out. We were all herded outside one morning to the drive in front of the main entrance and told to look up. I can see it now; the long, silver-grey airship that was known as the R101, sailing ponderously overhead and seeming to fill the whole sky. That must have been only weeks or days before its sad downfall, and the consequent loss of life.

I remember Empire Day, which was celebrated every spring, and one occasion when we were all dressed up in 'Empire' costumes, to say our piece to an audience of parents about the country we were representing. I was India, and resplendent in an orange sari lent by a friend of my parents who had lived there. "Doesn't she look sweet!" said the friend, and, confident that I deserved the epithet, I proclaimed my piece with aplomb.

Handsworth College was a fine building, which housed about sixty students training for the Methodist ministry, with courses in Theology, New and Old Testament studies, with Greek and Hebrew, and in church history. Each student had a bedroom and, on the ground floor, a small study with an open fireplace where he could light a coal fire. There were lecture-rooms, a library, a great hall and a tower from which, if you climbed the many steps, you could see the whole campus and well beyond. I remember standing, with as big a crowd as the space allowed, on top of the tower, watching an eclipse of the sun.

One summer, work was begun on building a chapel in the grounds. While the students were away for the long vacation, we children hung around the site in the evenings after the workmen had gone home, and played in the little trucks which carried sand and cement. It was a beautiful chapel when complete. I went in to watch a lady artist who had been engaged to paint a mural above the door, a copy of the Annunciation by Fra Angelico. I thought how wonderful it would be to have such a task.

We practised our 'spying' skills on the young men, watching them from behind bushes and flitting 'unseen' from tree to tree. They saw us of course, and would wave. Some of them were more friendly than others, and ready to chat. But we had strict instructions not to make nuisances of ourselves.

The students themselves tended the big cricket field, and would sometimes make use of the huge roller, which had a flat wooden structure over the top, with a handle at each corner and took four men to push and pull. One day they let me (probably being importunate) sit on the wooden frame for a ride. I carelessly dangled my leg over the side and caught my ankle in the axle of the roller. It was fortunate that the men stopped pushing as soon as my scream of pain rent the air. The ankle was badly crushed, and one of them lifted me down and carried me home. I was laid up for quite a while, but fortunately no great harm was done. I always associate the strong, distinctive smell of witch-hazel ointment with that incident. At the age of nine years, I fell in love with the young man who carried me home. His name was Mr Woodward, and he had flaxen hair.

Our house, like those of all the other college lecturers, entertained students for tea once a week in term time. The afternoon allotted to us was Friday, when four or five young men came to enjoy sandwiches and 'deadlies', as my father called the shop-bought iced cakes usually served up. One Friday I asked him who were coming that afternoon, and he told me their names. Among them was Mr Woodward and, unwisely and unguardedly, I exclaimed with glee, "Oh goody! I love Mr Woodward."

When we were all seated around the laden tea table, Dad recounted this outburst to the whole company, who found it hilarious and laughed heartily at my expense. For me there was no torture in the entire world worse than being laughed at, and I was mortified. How could Dad have so betrayed me? Oh! The perfidy of grown-ups! I tried, feebly to deny the words, but Grandma North was staying with us at the time, and reprimanded me sternly for 'telling lies'. But I was allowed to sit next to my idol, who kindly did his best to put me at my ease and keep me entertained. The poor man was most probably teased without mercy when they all got back to their quarters.

It is time I said something about drawing and painting. From the very beginning it was recognised that I had some talent in that direction, and I cannot think of a time when I did not regard it as an important part of my identity. I can understand why poets and artists of all kinds talk of a 'Muse'. It is as if one had a special friend, like those whom children conjure up for themselves, who is always there to fill one's head and guide one's hand. Although later in my life I tried to push him aside and ignore my Muse, he—yes I am sure it is a 'he'—would not lie quiet in the end.

I can remember a day at Miss Lowe's school when we had been told to draw a picture of a man slipping on a banana-skin, and a boy laughing. I have no idea where the teacher got such a subject, which might seem unsuitable for children, but it did lend itself to illustrative powers of action and expression. My drawing was held up for praise because, while all the others showed each item as a separate picture, unconnected, I had made a compact group, with the boy nearest and largest, slightly in front of the falling man, whose arms and legs were flailing. I had an inbuilt feel for composition.

When the weather was fine, we children were put into wellies and pushed out of doors to stay as long as possible while the housework was done. If it rained, on the other hand, we were allowed to go to the top floor where one of the rooms was ours. It started off as the 'nursery', but as we grew out of toddlerhood, the name was changed to 'the Sanctum', and Florence, our live-in maid, would carry buckets of coal up the two flights of stairs, to light a fire in the black hearth. Central heating was a rarity in those days. Nightly, I prayed that it would rain hard the next morning so that I could stay in the Sanctum and fill my drawing-book with pictures; and I lay in bed planning them. Perhaps it would be 'the Princess and the Frog' and I would do the princess reflected in the waters of a fountain. She would wear a dimity muslin veil which you could half-see through. I have painted such pictures many times since, and there is always some tit-bit of the visual world to present the artist with a pleasurable challenge.

The compulsion to draw did land me in trouble sometimes. I was severely reprimanded for using a pencil to draw on the wallpaper in my bedroom. I was obliged to clean it off as best I could, and promised never to do such a thing again. Alas! I broke my promise. The fireplace in the dining room was surrounded by a wide wooden mantelshelf and panelling. One day, using some sharp instrument, I scratched a face onto it. The following morning when I arrived at the breakfast table where the rest of the family were gathered, my father grimly confronted me and demanded to know if I was responsible for this vandalism of college property. Faced with the evidence, like George Washington I could not deny my culpability.

Whereupon Dad put me across his knee, pulled down my pants, and used the heel of his slipper to whack my bottom a number of times.

My mother was not present in the dining room. No doubt knowing what was coming, she could not face it and had found something to do in the kitchen. But my humiliation had been played out in front of my goggle-eyed siblings, and that hurt far more than my sore behind. Probably by today's rules my father was acting illegally, but he was never one to shirk an unpleasant task if he deemed it necessary, and I did not deface the walls again.

As far as I remember, that was the only time he used corporal punishment to discipline any of us, but he did confront me on other occasions. One evening, ready for bed, I came down to say 'Goodnight', and he asked the routine question, "Have you cleaned your teeth?"

"Yes", I said, lying through them.

There must have been something in the way I said it which gave me away, for, leaving me standing, he climbed the stairs and returned, holding my toothbrush.

"You lied to me Peggy", he said sternly, "You have not cleaned your teeth".

"How did you know?" I gasped.

"Your toothbrush is perfectly dry!" he said.

Once again I was forced to admit my guilt; but the wide-eyed, open-mouthed gaze I turned on him was not due to fear of reprisal —none actually came. It registered my stunned admiration for his detective powers, worthy of Sherlock Holmes himself!

Legends and fairy-tales were always my favourite reading, and have never been supplanted. My father bought a series of illustrated books for us. It was *Myth and Legend in Literature and Art*, and was intended for adults rather than children. Those copies have gone, but I have since been able to replace them all from second-hand bookshops. Classic, Teutonic, Celtic, Egyptian, Babylonian, Indian, and Tales of Chivalry; they are all there, and are still a delight and a valuable reference library.

When Grandma North died she could have had little to leave, but we were each presented with a volume from her collection. Mine was *Irish Fairy Tales*, published by MacMillan in 1920, written in what I can only describe as an enchanting Irish brogue by the poet James Stephens, and illustrated by Arthur Rackham. I curled up with it and was lost to everything else. For days I lived in the Celtic Otherworld with Fionn McUail, and I love him still. I still have the book, though it got tattered and had to be rebound.

Arthur Rackham and Edmund Dulac were the celebrated illustrators of those days, and I think they have never been surpassed. I also have *The Rubaiyat of Omar Khayam* which Dulac illustrated, and that too is a great source of inspiration. In both books the illustrations are mounted carefully on the page, and covered with a layer of tissue paper, as if they are treasures to be treated with respect, as they should be; indeed, as is the whole book, a work of art.

Every month we received, and pounced upon, the newest edition of Arthur Mee's *Treasure House* magazine, a lavishly illustrated encyclopaedic type of periodical containing a wealth of information about almost everything, and well worth keeping and binding at the end of the year. When I look at the magazines which my granddaughters favour nowadays, they seem to me so shallow and frivolous, all about fashion, boys and pop-idols. "But", say their parents reasonably, "they help the girls to grow up and make their entry into teens and adulthood".

No doubt they are right. We had far too little of that kind of education, and I was very ignorant of anything to do with sex or the world outside until I was in my twenties. Any kind of self-enhancement, or 'showing-off', was treated with cool suspicion, and I was especially discouraged as being already, "too full of myself".

Florence, our maid-of-all-work (I don't know if I ever heard her surname) was a large woman and a strong personality, much stronger than my mother who, I think, regarded her with awe. She found her a reliable and welcome prop, but feared her forthrightness and bowed to her opinions in matters domestic. Florence was in no way indulgent towards us younger members of the household, though she was expected to call us 'Master Chris' and 'Miss Peggy', a title which I accepted awkwardly and which I'm sure she resented.

We were sent after dinner to the kitchen to help dry the washing-up, while Florence stood at the sink with her brawny arms in the suds. I am certain that she purposely made us wait a long time standing about with our tea towels at the ready, while she washed all the saucepans and cooking utensils which required no drying, before tackling the china and cutlery. In some strange way she was levelling the ground between the dining-room company and the kitchen, and enjoying her power. We grumbled amongst ourselves but never dared to confront her.

When I grew to teenage, she became increasingly jealous, and was so rude to me that at last I rebelled. Not wishing, or daring, to cause a domestic crisis, I bore it for years and never answered back. After a particularly outrageous insult in my late teens, I reported it to my father and Florence was gone within the week to work in a munitions factory for the war effort.

My father's first pastoral charge when he left training college, was St John's Methodist church in Bangor, and he always felt a strong affection for North Wales. Nearly every year we spent part of the summer holidays on the Welsh coast, usually Bangor or Llanfair-fechan or Colwyn Bay. Dad loved tramping over the hills, which he had come to know well, and he would take Chris and myself on long climbs around the Ogwen Pass up to the Devil's Kitchen and the Glyder Fach and Glyder Fawr. We climbed Snowdon and grew to love the area.

Boarding houses and landladies are rare these days, but we always stayed in a large house on the sea front, where we occupied the bedrooms on the first floor, and had a sitting room. We would arrive back, wet or sandy or both, after a strenuous day on hills or beach, and be served a good home-cooked meal by the landlady, as if we were round the dining table at home. I remember the sunsets spreading glory over the Menai Straits.

My sister Bronwen, who owed her name to Dad's love of the Welsh coast, made her appearance when I was eight, so she was only small when my mother fell seriously ill, in her forties. It was some fatal germ that attacked her heart, and she lay in the big bedroom at Handsworth, surrounded with pillows. We children, of course, were ignorant of the gravity of the situation, and had often seen her stricken with sickness and headaches. One evening we were looked after by Miss Johnson, the housekeeper to the college Principal, Dr Lofthouse, who was a widower. She came to tuck me up and wish me 'Goodnight', after I had gone to bed. She bent down and patted my head, and said with feeling, "Oh! You poor little thing". Suddenly my world did a somersault, and my mind added up the evidence. She meant I was 'poor' because Mummy was dying! She was going to die! I found it hard to go to sleep that night, but as children will, I did drop off and woke next morning with a mind that would not accept such dire news until it actually happened, and perhaps not entirely even then.

By this time my brother Chris was a pupil at Kingswood, the Methodist boarding school for boys, founded by John Wesley himself, at Bath in Somerset. I had left Miss Lowe's and was walking every morning through Handsworth Park to Soho Road to attend the King Edward Grammar School for girls. There I sat, somewhat lost and bemused at the back of a very large class, and struggled to take in what was being written on the blackboard. But I was in my element in the art class, and the very stroppy art teacher who did not hold back the most caustic criticism of untalented work, gave me the art prize at the end of the one year I spent there.

One day when I was twelve years old, my father came to me in the Sanctum where I was amusing myself with a pencil as usual, and asked:

"How would you like to go to boarding school, Peggy?"

Exciting tales of hockey triumphs and midnight feasts in the dorm sprang into my mind. I had also read the more popular children's literature as well as the myths and legends.

"Yes please!" I said, unhesitatingly, which must have made my father a little sad, but relieved too. My brother had settled into Kingswood and I was going to present no difficulty.

So there followed days of buying and fitting, mending and packing and stitching on of Cash's nametapes to every possible article. My trunk was sent off P.L.A. (Passenger's Luggage in Advance) and at last I stood by my mother's bedside in all my new finery, to say goodbye. She, poor gentle soul, no doubt knew that it was the last time we would ever see one another. She lay inert on her pillows and the tears poured down her face. I must have felt something of the gravity of the situation or the scene would not remain so vividly in my mind after all these years. But my head could not—or would not—entertain any thought so final; and besides, outside that sad room a huge adventure was waiting for me. So, dry-eyed, I kissed her and went to meet it.

Three

School Days

TRINITY Hall School, or T.H. as I came to know it, was the girls' equivalent of Wesley's Kingswood, and all the pupils were daughters of Methodist ministers. It was situated in Southport on the Lancashire coast, and I travelled by train from Snow Hill station in Birmingham, changing once at Crewe. A friend of my father, stationed in the Birmingham area, had three daughters who attended the school. Their names were, neatly, Monica, Jessica, and Veronica. I was put into the charge of the eldest of the three, Monica, who promised to look after me until we reached our destination, where school staff would meet us.

Only now, as I go over these events in my head, do I appreciate the calmness, care and consideration with which my father made arrangements for our future, at a time which was so traumatic for him. I'm sorry Dad. Let me record my heartfelt 'thank you' here, so many years too late.

I had only been in school about three weeks when the head-mistress of the Junior school, Miss Lobb, sent for me one morning and told me very gently that my mother had died. Now at last I had to face the truth, and I wept bitterly. After a while Miss Lobb sent for Monica who was once again given charge of me, and we were told that we need not attend lessons that morning, but could go for a walk, just the two of us, so that I could have some time to come to terms with the news. So we went to the beach, the wide, wide stretch of sands, where in Southport the tide rarely, if ever, comes in.

My father deemed it would be unwise to disturb my period of settling into a new school, so I did not go home for the funeral, but he came to visit me a few weeks later and took me out and talked. Children such as I do not take long to put sad things behind them and look to the future, and that's how it was with me.

T.H. consisted of two buildings, the Senior and Junior schools, about a mile apart—or so it seems to me in retrospect. I was twelve years old, so did not start with the first class, Form Three, but with the Second, the Remove. I have never found out to this day why classes were called so, or why it was necessary to have a class with such an odd name between Forms 3 and 4, but so it was, and it seemed natural to me at the time because I had read school stories in which the heroines came from the Remove.

There were about half a dozen of us to a dormitory, of varying ages, the eldest being appointed 'head'. In each dormitory, curtains surrounded the beds in order to provide some privacy for dressing and undressing, as in a hospital ward. One pillow lay on each bed, and a rough grey blanket, maybe two in winter. A small chest of drawers at the side was for all our clothes and possessions.

Over white blouses we wore navy serge gym-tunics, buttoned at the shoulder and pleated. The pleats had to be pressed with a hot iron over a damp cloth before term began, but they soon lost their sharp edge. The children in the younger classes wore their new tunics practically to their ankles, but by the time the same girls had reached the Upper Sixth at the age of eighteen, those garments were like mini-skirts, long before Mary Quant made such things fashionable. Our long legs, clad in black woollen stockings, held up with a suspender belt (no tights in those days), were as exposed as those of chorus girls. Methodist ministers were not lavishly paid, and the school governors knew they must make allowances for that. The seat of my gym tunic was diligently patched and darned before I finally cast it off for good.

Every Saturday morning there was a 'mending hour', when our garments came back from the laundry and we had to darn the holes in our black stockings. For undergarments, each girl wore a 'liberty bodice', a short button-up top with suspenders attached, until it was decided she needed a bra. We were all obliged to wear thick navy bloomers with elastic at waist and thigh, and pockets in them for a handkerchief.

It is time I added something more to that coat of arms I am planning, and it shall be a chevron design in blue and yellow stripes, for at T.H. we wore a tie of those colours and they decorated the band around our black velour hats.

For the convenience of staff and, I imagine, for economic reasons, all the lessons, Senior and Junior, were held in the Junior School, and the whole school gathered in the dining-room there for the mid-day meal. Every class of older girls also had a room in the Senior building, but generally the upper school walked, in twos or threes, to the Junior building every morning, and back in the evening. I remember how we loitered back sometimes on winter evenings after dark had fallen, and looked out for warm, firelit scenes in the uncurtained windows of houses along the way. How nice it would be to be going home to tea in front of the fire with the family.

For class occasions, such as a visit to the local swimming baths or the playing field or the regular Saturday afternoon walk, we were herded in 'crocodile', two by two, with a mistress in charge. The prize position, much competed for at such times, was that of leaders in the front. The worst place to be landed with was at the back, accompanying the mistress with whom we were expected to make polite conversation.

Every morning at seven, a raucous handbell made its insistent clamour outside the dormitory door, and we had half an hour to haul ourselves out of deep sleep and bed, wash and pull on our clothes before going downstairs to take our places at the breakfast table. I invariably arrived unwashed, unbuttoned, with suspenders and shoes unfastened, my girdle round my neck instead of my waist, and still knotting my tie. Oh! The lure of the warm blankets on a cold winter's morning!

The diet was satisfying and much healthier than many school meals today, but it was always the same. One knew what day it was by the dinner menu: roast on Sunday ("eat up your greens"), mince on Monday, stew on Wednesday, fish-cakes on Friday, sausage-and-mash on Saturday. We were required to take a pot of jam with us at the beginning of every term, labelled with our name. Wise girls rationed their helpings from the start. The rest of us had to eat plain bread and butter for tea for the second half of the term.

Enhancing one's person was not encouraged. No make-up or jewellery was ever allowed. Employees of a nearby hairdressing establishment were called in twice a term to cut and wash our hair, and the whole operation was conducted on a conveyor-belt system. In the basement was a long row of wash-basins, and we queued up for our turn. After a cut, which in my case was a straight bob and fringe, we were sat before a basin with a towel around our necks, and the hairdressers—usually men and not remarkable for their gentle touch—dunked our heads in the water with a firm hand on the back of the neck. The shampoo used had an extremely strong tar content and the smell clung to our heads for days afterwards. No doubt it was intended to kill unwelcome squatters, and it would have discouraged the hardiest creatures if a drop in the eye were anything to go by.

Released, we stood towelling our scalps and combing them, under the penetrating eye of Miss R, the housekeeper, a woman of so grim and sour an expression that she could have put Grandma North clean out of countenance. It seemed to be her cherished purpose in life to ensure that no girl attempted to prink or titivate in any way. Should anyone dare try to make a little wave in her coiffure, Miss R would pounce, pull out and confiscate the 'kirbygrip'.

My hair was strong, thick and very straight. My granddaughters nowadays have special combs to smooth out any kinks or waves. Today's style of long, straight hair would have suited me splendidly, but in those days we all yearned for waves and curls, and envied those who came away from the washing ordeal with a natural, curly mop.

My best features were my eyes, big and brown like my mother's. I was teased in a friendly way for having a long neck. Though I did not know it, I would have made a good subject for a Modigliani painting. My worst worry was my legs, which would sprout dark hair all over like a man's. I could get no advice on how to deal with them, and indeed did not know who or how to ask for it. The only depilatory that I dared to try, secretly, once in my teens, stank the whole house out and brought embarrassing questions and cries of protest and disgust from the rest of the household. On top of all that, I was hampered by the implanted idea that any attempt at personal enhancement was immodest and sinful. Nice girls did not give endless thought to their appearance.

But nothing dampened my spirits for long. I loved T.H. and I shone there. In classes much smaller than those of King Edward Grammar School, Birmingham, I flourished and triumphed. In maths I was still not much good, though I did well in geometry—it's all shapes and forms anyway. Not very convincing at conversational language like French, I shone in Latin which was visual reading and like a word puzzle. At English I took prizes and always had a big part in any dramatic performances we put on. Because I was taller than average and had a contralto voice, I was invariably cast in a man's part—Orlando in 'As You Like It', and, to my delight, Shylock in 'Merchant of Venice'.

For one Christmas, the music teacher produced 'The Mummers' Play'. Dressed in medieval costume, we mummers (of whom I was the chief spokesman) carried lanterns made of jam-jars painted black on one side, and given handles made of string. Each had a candle, and scenes were lit up by setting our lanterns in a semi-circle on the ground, light side turned to the action, leaving the rest of the stage in darkness. So, in turn, we lit up the manger scene, the shepherds on the hillside, a feast, when a Welsh girl named Dilys came in bearing a magnificent boar's head bedecked with bay and rosemary. She sang the carol in a good clear voice. It was a great success and we performed it in the local church. The Methodist church—also called 'Trinity'—was next door to the Senior School, and is probably there still, though T.H. itself was closed down long ago. We attended the service every Sunday morning, and must have filled a sizeable number of pews.

I remember one year when I was sixteen, each of the senior classes was told to produce some dramatic item. All three would be performed one night in the school, and one would be chosen for performance in the church hall. By class election, I was captain of the Fifth at that time and was expected to, 'come up with something'. I wrote a humorous play based on a standard Grimm's fairy-tale theme. The princess in the play was under an evil spell, whereby her cooking was so dire that any dish concocted by her was death to the consumer. The King, her father, therefore proclaimed that she would become the wife (with the obligatory half of his kingdom as dowry) of any man who could eat one of her suet puddings and survive. There were, of course, three brothers, princes, of whom the two elder were unwisely rude to a witch and received no help from her. The youngest, in the usual way, was rewarded for his courtesy with a loan of the hag's cat, which had an iron constitution and could eat anything, unscathed.

There was a grand scene, when the two arrogant suitors ate the pudding and died, horribly and spectacularly, and had to be carried out on a stretcher, to delighted cheering from our audience. The youngest prince kept diverting everyone's attention, while he fed the pudding to the cat hidden under the table. So he won the day and the princess.

I played the hero—and no! I did not cast myself: I would have preferred to be the witch. The parts were allotted very democratically, and everyone had a part to play. The whole performance was greeted with noisy acclaim, and, in pink doublet and hose, I took my bow to cries of "Author! Author!" Our class was chosen to perform in the church hall, though the reception there was nothing like as ecstatic as it was from our schoolmates. Was it any wonder that I was happy at school?

I recommend the theme of our play to producers of pantomime. It could make a welcome change from the Cinderellas and Dick Whittingtons served up year after year.

One Speech Day my father came and watched as I had to ascend the platform five or six times to receive various awards from the hands of an elderly superstar of the Methodist hierarchy. On the fifth occasion he exclaimed, "What, you again!" In the entertainment that followed I was taking part with one classmate in a lively sketch, all in French, as a garrulous, hen-pecking wife who got her come-uppance from her downtrodden little husband. When I joined him afterwards, my father looked somewhat dazed.

"I didn't know you could do it, Peggy", he said. My cup was full and running over!

In the dormitory that night I drew the curtains of my cubicle around me and knelt beside the bed, as I had been taught to do since infancy. I thought I was 'giving thanks'. In truth I was riding along on a heady wave of triumphant excitement. If I had ignored the sound of clapping in my head and listened, I might have heard the Almighty saying in a voice remarkably like that of my father, "Peggy, you are too full of yourself by half! Hubris is an unlovely trait." But in spite of all my awards, I would never have won a prize for listening.

At the end of two terms every year, we had tests or internal exams. In the six years that I spent at T.H., I managed to keep first place each time. The results were read out in front of the whole school, and I would have been mortified if my name had not headed the list. I had to work hard for it, but, having established my place at the beginning, I could not bear the thought of losing it.

When I was sixteen, along with everyone else in my year, I sat the school certificate examination, in which, if one did well enough, one gained matriculation, the passport to a college course. I took ten or so subjects and passed them all well enough, with distinctions in art and botany. The last was a surprise, but I reckon my ability to draw specimens tipped the balance there.

I have been asked fairly recently if we had our hockey triumphs, and if there ever really were midnight feasts in the dorm. We played hockey during the winter and spring terms, sometimes on the bare wide sands of Southport beach, with icy winds forcing us into action, just to keep from freezing solid. I was not a keen sportswoman, though I did play in the teams against other schools, and enjoyed being a goal-scoring member of the netball team. I took my bronze and silver medals in swimming at the baths, though I had to grit my teeth and close my eyes before diving off the top board. During the silver test, we had to swim a mile in full clothing, which meant wearing our black woollen stockings attached to a suspender belt. My suspender broke, and I had to do half the length breast-stroke, with one hand holding up the stocking. No part of the clothing could be shed until all was accomplished, and then we had to carry it all to the side of the bath.

No, I did not really enjoy sport, and have never joined any team or club since I left school.

As for midnight feasts, the answer is 'Yes'. I can remember one feast we had, towards the end of term before we all broke up for the holidays. It took a lot of organising. For a start it was not easy to get provisions secretly, but we found ways. If one of us had a visit from a relative who would take her out on the town, that was the easiest way to obtain food. We did not readily have access to funds. A ten-shilling pocket-money allowance was handed in to the authorities at the beginning of term, and would have to last until the end, doled out sparingly, only for a legitimate reason. Letters to parents sometimes brought small parcels, but even letters might be subjected to scrutiny. We wrote home each week, but had to hand in the envelopes unsealed.

I don't remember what dishes we had for our illicit feast, except that I was sent some jelly cubes, and had to find a way of making them into edible jellies without discovery by anyone in authority. The first question was: 'What could I make them in?' Down in the basement, where we packed and unpacked our trunks and kept our sports gear, there were storage shelves, and I noticed some dark-green flowerpots of the sort to hold an aspidistra plant. They were just the job and I managed to 'borrow' a couple on two occasions, and smuggle them up to the dormitory under my coat. So far so good!

On retiring at night we walked along the corridor from dormitory to bathroom where there was a plentiful supply of really hot water. To get there one would have to pass the mistress on duty, so the pots went, one at a time, under a towel, and were brought back to the dorm with the dissolved jelly-cubes inside. Having no measuring jug I had to guess at a pint of water, but three toothmugsful about did it. The pots were left under my bed for the jellies to set, and I had to hope that no-one would clean or inspect there before nightfall. What we did for spoons I cannot remember or imagine, but it was undoubtedly fun! Of course, it was the clandestine nature of the enterprise that gave our feast its appeal.

I was the special pet of Miss B, the art teacher, and she put me in for every competition going, so I won things like a voucher, to be spent in a Southport art shop, or books on famous artists. Every year, even while I was in Primary School, I had taken one of the Royal Drawing Society's examinations. These were a nationwide institution, and were graded one to six. I think I had passed two or three grades before I went to T.H., and Miss B arranged for me to carry on.

The Society produced a printed pamphlet each year, with reproductions of the best entries from all over Britain and beyond. Grade Five was all about light and shade, and we were asked to draw, in pencil, a moonlit scene in which one figure was playing on pipes, and another dancing. Miss B, during an art class, proudly produced the R.D.S. pamphlet and passed it round the class. It was the first time I ever saw one of my pictures in print.

The following year I took the last grade, Number Six. This concentrated on illustration and historical costume. I had to paint a watercolour entitled 'The court jester makes a mistake', and we were expected to indicate the century in which our picture was set. Mine was in the fifteenth century, and showed two haughty ladies, in elaborate head-dresses, looking decidedly offended as they swept past a very red and embarrassed jester. It won me the Ablett prize for that year, a gold medal, which I have long ago lost; I am not good at keeping such things.

After matriculation I was faced with a choice. What was I going to do now? The three or four subjects I would choose for the advanced examination would depend on what I hoped to take up as a career. Miss B told me that I could easily get a scholarship to the Slade School of Art in London, and it seemed a wonderful prospect. I remember going to my father's study to ask his advice. I told him about my inclination to do art, but asserted that I did not want to end up teaching it in a school. In that I am sure I was right; I would have made a poor art teacher. I might have taught other subjects, but in the matter of art I find it difficult to let other people get on with it in their own way. I always want to pick up the brush and do it myself, and that won't do!

My father was of the opinion that, in that case, I had better keep art as a hobby, and enjoy it. In his judgement I would never be able to earn a decent living out of just producing pictures. I was happy in other subjects, so choose something else.

Not surprisingly, Religious Instruction had been given a prominent place in the T.H. curriculum, taught by Miss Lobb herself, and

I had always done well in it. I decided that, if it could not be art then I would take up theology and do what my father had once set out to do, become a missionary. I am not the first artist by a long way to be torn between those two subjects. Van Gogh had the same problem, and look what happened to him!

Thus art was dropped from my timetable from that year on. I don't know if Miss B ever forgave me. For the two years spent in the Sixth Form I took Latin, English (language and literature), History and Greek, starting that last subject from scratch. I passed in all four subjects, and was ready for college. Dad had a word with the powers-that-be, and it was arranged that I should live at home, attending the lectures at Handsworth College, the only woman student along-side a college full of men. I would take the three-year course, ending in a B.A. degree from Birmingham University.

By this time my father had remarried, and we had a stepmother. Her name was Helen Winter, and she was the only daughter of a courtly Scottish gentleman who owned a shop and restaurant in Birmingham, and a factory that produced a popular currant loaf called 'Harvo'. They had a large house in Sutton Coldfield called 'Good Hope'. It had extensive grounds, with a lake and fields and rows of greenhouses. Sometimes on Sundays the chauffeur-driven car would take us there for lunch, when we were served with dishes by a maid, and there were finger-bowls on the table. We young ones had to watch warily what the adults did, and carefully copy them to get it right.

Dad was married to Helen Winter when I was fifteen, and I was the only bridesmaid, my brother Chris playing the part of Best Man. We were all asked to call her 'Mother', and we did, but we did not accept her as wholeheartedly as I think she would have liked. I know she tried hard, but it can be an uneasy relationship, especially with teenagers. My stepbrother, Richard, was born a year later.

In the meantime, my father added to his honours by taking a Doctorate in Divinity, and contributing articles to a number of Biblical commentaries and other publications. His big work, on the passage in the book of Isaiah known as Deutero-Isaiah, became a standard textbook among theological students. A decade or so later, he told me proudly one day that his name had appeared in 'The Times' birthday list. In my ignorance I was less impressed than he perhaps hoped or deserved.

My brother Chris became a botanist and went to Reading University to take his degree. My two sisters, Barbara and Bronwen, had followed me to T.H. At eighteen I said goodbye to school and prepared to take my place in the lecture rooms of Handsworth College.

Little happened during the first two years of my college career. Every morning I walked with my father across to the main entrance and mingled with the men, who soon got used to my presence. I did not fall in love with any of them, or they with me, but I got on well enough with the group who were doing the same course as myself. I missed out on college social life, and in the afternoons when my fellow-students played cricket or football, I went for long walks around the Handsworth area.

I went through all the common fits of angst and unreasonableness to which teenagers have ever been subject, and my father and stepmother bore them patiently. Once when I was in a black mood, which I could not explain to myself let alone them, Dad asked if I would like to go to a concert with them to chase away the doldrums. They took me to the concert hall in the city centre, and we heard a performance of Elgar's 'Dream of Gerontius'. It blew my mind and put my silly blues in their place; I have loved it ever since.

I feel that the escutcheon that I am planning must bear some symbol of Handsworth College, which played such a part in my life. The college itself had a coat of arms, but the only item I can remember in it was an emu-like bird. On enquiry I was told that it was a cassowary, which probably owed its place to a rhyme by Anon:

> "Behold the cassowary, on the plains of Timbuktu,
> It will eat the missionary, hat and gloves and
> hymnbook too".

I think my informant had his tongue well lodged in his cheek, but I will reserve a place on my shield for a cassowary bird.

Towards the end of my second year, and after I had reached my twenty-first birthday and was, officially at least, an adult, the national news was heavy with rumblings and threats of war. Naively, we rejoiced when Neville Chamberlain came home from his meeting with Hitler, and it seemed the worst might be averted. But the day came when we were all gathered round the wireless to hear the voice of the Prime Minister say, "We are now at war with Germany".

We remembered the first Great War, only twenty-one years before, which our parents had experienced and of which we younger ones had heard such harrowing accounts. It was the same enemy, and the same thing happening all over again. In our circle, we thought of my brother Chris, just twenty-two.

But for the year following, the 'phoney war' made it all seem like a bad dream. Little happened and life went on as usual, except that we collected our gas masks and carried them around, and after a while rationing came in for food and clothes. I had one more year of studies before taking my degree. After that, the college would be closed and my father would be posted elsewhere. I must decide what to do and where to go next.

The North family on a day out by the Thames in Middlesex, *c.*1922
with me seated centre, my brother Christopher on the left
and my sister Barbara on father's knee.

'Tranby', the North family house in Friary Road, Handsworth Wood,
Birmingham, *c.* mid-1920s to 1940.

Mother and myself in the gardens at Tranby,
*c.*1920s and 1930s.

Barbara playing 'French cricket' with children.
Handsworth College in background.

A hammock full—from left, myself, Bronwen, the girl from next door (Margaret Howard), and Barbara.

Myself and friend sitting below a pear tree and nearby, the revolving summerhouse.

The gardeners—Mr Beddoes, flanked by Mr Hickman, his assistant (hatted), and son, George.

The Methodist Training College, Handsworth Wood, Birmingham.

A party of students from the College to tea in the garden—
a Friday afternoon ritual (revolving summerhouse on the right).
Mother, Barbara and myself in the group.

The North family as it developed: from left,
Christopher, Bronwen, Mother, myself,
Father and Barbara, *c*.1927.

Part Two

HOME AND AWAY

HOME AND AWAY

❧

Four

Love and War

I HAD a degree of sorts, but it would be of little use without some more practical qualification. I would need at some time to take a teacher training diploma, but I could not ask my father to finance that just then; his future was as questionable as my own. Besides, there was a war going on, and I felt I should be doing my bit. I decided to go on a short training course, a week's lessons and a period working on a ward in a hospital, and join the Civil Nursing Reserve. Accordingly, when I had taken all the necessary steps, I was drafted to a hospital in Stafford.

There were no patients in the hospital, which was set up and waiting for casualties when they began to arrive from the front. We nurses were all billeted out around the town in private houses. At first we filled in our time cleaning already clean wards, rolling bandages and getting in more training. Under the guidance of a nurse who, in civilian life, was a member of the Birmingham Repertory Company, we put on plays and entertainment for—I can't remember whom. She chose me to play Matron in a skit about hospital life, and I followed the poor woman around as often as I could, surreptitiously noting all her idiosyncrasies and copying them. I must have been the only nurse who had the cheek!

Casualties came in eventually, and we were busy. But there was a strong rumour going round that anyone in medicine would be obliged to stay in that profession for the duration of the war. We would all be conscripted. We untrained auxiliary nurses were at the bottom of the pecking order, and had to do all the cleaning and sluicing jobs. I didn't mind that, but I was not interested in the profession enough to want to take it up and work for my State Registered Nurse qualification. It began to look as if the war might last a lot longer than everyone had at first thought, and I knew that hospitals were not where I wanted to make my career. I was keen to get my teaching diploma. So, after nearly a year in Stafford, I wrote to the Methodist Mission Board and offered my services.

My offer was accepted and I was told to turn up at Kingsmead College, Selly Oak, Birmingham. I could have a term of general training and start a course of Teacher Training in the autumn. So, once again I packed my bags and arrived at Kingsmead on 1st May, 1941. I was about a week late, for the Summer Term had already started. All the sleeping quarters in the college itself were already taken by other students, so I was boarded in the spare room at the home of the chief warden and his family.

There were, I think, about twenty students, a few Methodist men and a number of young women. There was also a group of five Welshmen, Presbyterians, all destined for the Welsh mission-field in Assam, and all in their last term of training. Their names were George Morgan, Trebor Thomas, Meirion Lloyd, Merfyn Jones, and Basil Jones.

Only later did I hear from Basil of his reaction to my coming. The day after my arrival when we were gathered in the common room, he was watching me intently. One of the wardens who had been watching him strolled over to him and said: "You shouldn't look at a girl like that!" Basil turned to him and declared, "I'm going to marry her!" He never was slow at making up his mind, as I would learn.

I was unaware of this conversation, but I encountered the 'look' the next day. I had met men who aimed to seduce with their skills or charm with their chat-line and been mildly amused, but subjected to that look I curled up inside and melted like an ice-cream left out in the sun.

After that our eyes sought one another whenever we were in a room together. A few days later I was talking with a group of girls about entertainment in the city. I learned that, in spite of the war, there were still some worthwhile shows in the theatres. There was, for instance, a performance of 'Hansel and Gretel', the Humperdinck opera, at the Birmingham Rep. I had seen it before and been enchanted. It was the only piece of theatre to which my mother had taken us as children.

"I'd love to go to that", I said. Almost immediately Basil was at my shoulder. "Will you let me take you to that opera?" he asked.

I needed no persuading. We took the bus one evening and settled into our seats. I loved it—as magic as ever. But not all the magic came from the stage. I don't know how much of the performance Basil saw; he was swivelled round sideways in his seat most of the time so that he could hold both my willing hands in his.

When it was over we wandered out in a dream, oblivious of everything and everyone except each other. Coiled round one another in a kind of Celtic knot, we stepped into a busy Birmingham street. The traffic screeched to a halt on either side, leaving a pathway for us, and we made our way like the Israelites crossing the Red Sea, but with none of their urgency, until a frustrated lorry driver leant out of his cab and shouted in a voice thick with disgust, "Why don't you SIT in the road!" We came to our senses, dashed for the opposite kerb, and collapsed, laughing, all without letting go of one another.

In the days that followed, we spent as much time together as we could glean from our timetables. I was only filling in a term with odd lectures before starting a serious course in the autumn, but Bas was in the throes of his final studies. Yet the evenings were largely ours, and we made the most of them. It was obvious to everyone else that we were what today is called, 'an item'.

But the College, it seemed, had a principle. It did not house partners, wives or sweethearts at one time under its roof. We were threatening the orderly calm of the institution. One evening, Miss M, the warden in charge of female students, nobbled me and steered me round the gardens while suggesting that this relationship with a fellow-student was unwise, and I should, as she put it, 'slow down'. My father, who was now posted as minister to a Methodist Church in Leeds, was still on the committee of the College. It might be best, urged Miss M, if I were to go home for the rest of that term, to think about my situation and talk things over with him. I could go and pack right there and then and leave in the morning.

I was stunned! Bas was leaving at the end of that term, and possibly would be sent off to India before I could see him again. There had still been no commitment made between us in words; he had not proposed or asked me to marry him. To my mind that was irrelevant. I took it for granted that he wanted such a commitment as much as I did, and words were unnecessary. My true love had my heart, and I had his, as the poet says: "There never was a better bargain driven". I knew that no man in his position would act as he was doing unless marriage was his intent. Things were so much simpler than they are now, and I knew where I could put my trust. So I never hesitated but sought him out straight away and told him of my talk with Miss M.

He set his face grimly, urged me not to worry, and went to find her. He told me afterwards that he found her in the company of her sister, who was also on the staff. He himself was with another Welshman, Trebor Thomas, and they agreed that Trebor should engage the sister while Basil tackled Miss M. He used straight talking. She was totally out of touch with the world he said, and had no right to interrupt our happiness and growing companionship, which she had jeopardised with her interference.

I did not go home, but wrote to my father who replied saying that it would do the Selly Oak establishment no harm to have a 'bit of a shaking up', and I had his blessing. Of course he had not met Basil, but I had informed him in my letter that the new love of my life had two degrees, and had taken honours in Hebrew and Old Testament. So he couldn't be unsuitable, even if he was a Presbyterian—and a Welshman!

Basil's powers of oratory must have been considerable. We later heard that, after we had both left Kingsmead at the end of that term, Miss M had resigned from the college and gone to work among women in a factory. She felt she was, 'out of touch with the real world'.

At twenty-seven, Basil did have B.A., B.D. after his name, degrees from Cardiff and Aberystwyth, and his teacher's diploma. He was about three inches taller than I was, with hazel eyes and brown hair swept back off a high forehead; and he had a rather seductive deep speaking voice. What more could a girl ask for?

Our relationship flourished, and I went about in a daze. As a protégé of the Methodists, I was earmarked for service in China, and I was having regular face-to-face tutorials with an expert on that country, a Dr Foster, knowing full well that I was now destined, not for China but for India, with Basil. Dr Foster knew it too, but we carried on with the talks just the same and he introduced me to the male and female concept of Yang and Yin that I found fascinating. Of course I would not now be staying on after that term, or taking that elusive teacher training diploma. The Methodists were paying for me as their future employee. I learned later that the Presbyterian Mission Board came to an agreement with them, and paid back what had been spent on me for that summer term. So I was bought and sold, you might say!

For me, the rest of that May and June were a dream time. I had been told by the wife of the Chief Warden in whose house I was quartered, that I was welcome to use the kettle in their kitchen if I wished, to make myself a drink at any time; one day I filled it and lit the ring beneath it. I then went off and found quite different thoughts to occupy my mind, completely forgetting the kettle. The lady of the house rescued it much later, with a large hole burnt in the bottom of it. I felt very guilty and decided I must spend some of my meagre pocket money to buy them a new kettle, it was the least I could do. As I was hovering outside the local ironmongers, Basil found me and came inside to help me choose the new kettle. At the end of term concert, the college wag read out a humorous diary of the term's events. One item in June read, "Peggy burnt a hole in the Warden's kettle. What could she have been thinking of?"

I do not remember parting with Bas at the end of term. It would not be long before we saw one another again, for it was generally understood between us that each must visit the other's home and family before we were married, probably at the end of September. Before that, Basil was ordained as a minister of the Presbyterian Church in a ceremony which took place in Pont-y-clun, near Llan-trisant. Then he came to Leeds and was introduced.

My father could be somewhat intimidating and formidable, but Basil was not one to be cowed. He and I were remarkably alike in many ways, we were both strong, independent characters, with a marked aversion to bowing before anyone, however exalted. In Dad's presence, Bas tended to bridle and put up his defences, but in general he was warmly welcomed and well received into the family. The two of us took picnic food and went for long tramps on the Yorkshire moors. We kissed among the heather and went to Harrogate to buy an engagement ring. Then I travelled back with him to meet his family. Basil came from the Aberdare Valley in South Wales, from a mining village called Penrhiwceiber—very different from the big house in the grounds of Handsworth College. I confess that I had a slight shock when I first saw the tiny front in Station Terrace, with a door straight onto the pavement, one lower window and two above. Flecks of coal dust floated always in the air, and the mine dominated the village.

Basil's father (Farv) was a dark-eyed, curly-haired shoe-smith, who had worked with the ponies in the pit. His mother had been a dressmaker, and her word was the one that carried weight in the household. Basil was their only son, and he was adored. If they tended to indulge him it was understandable. Basil had contracted polio in his teens, and bore an operation scar on his left shoulder; he could not lift that arm above it. It says much for his strength of character that he passed through the school examinations to reach college, while going through such an ordeal, and his mother's pride in him was evident. I teased him wickedly, when I saw that she not only sugared his cup of tea, but also carefully stirred it before putting it into his hands.

He had two sisters, Rene, the elder, and Myra, who was younger than her brother. Rene was married and was staying in the house in Penrhiwceiber with her two small children, a boy and a girl, as evacuees from their home in the dangerous south-east of England, where the German bombing was growing more intense.

I don't know what they made of me, with my plummy English accent and my boarding-school background. I am sure that I was not the kind of girl they had imagined for their son, but we soon got on pretty well, and they made sacrifices to accommodate me. I was given the best bedroom and sank into a deeply-yielding feather mattress, until I was almost lost to sight!

Basil and I were married on 27th September, 1941, at the Methodist chapel in Roundhay, Leeds. In wartime, it was a modest affair. My father performed the service and I was 'given away' by my step-mother. I had managed to acquire extra clothing coupons to buy a dress—not long and white which would have been no use to me afterwards—and I could not afford anything useless. It was pink silk, calf-length. My sisters were present, but I had no bridesmaid. I had to walk down the aisle in intimidating silence, because the organist was very late turning up. He had been on Air Raid Patrol

(ARP) duty the previous night. The wedding cake was coated with dark brown chocolate, because white icing-sugar was impossible to come by. Any photographs were snap-shots taken by my father. After a week's honeymoon in York, we went back to Penrhiwceiber and Basil taught in the local primary school while we waited for a passage to India. It took six months to come, and when at last he was given his instructions, it was obvious that he was to go alone. No overseas travel was sanctioned for civilians and wives. There was little time for preparation, only a few days, and only necessary directions were given; it was all very 'hush-hush'. "Careless talk costs lives" warned the posters.

We had our last night together in a hotel in Liverpool, and on a cold, dank morning in March I tearfully kissed him 'goodbye', and strained my eyes to follow him as he disappeared into the mist around the dockside to board a ship whose name was not divulged. Not even Dido, watching as Aeneas sailed away, was more desolate than I! We would not see one another again for nearly three years.

So, left on my own I had to find a job. Neither the Methodists nor the Presbyterians would be interested in paying for my further training now, and my father was no longer responsible for me. Besides, as a wife I would not need qualification for any other occupation; that's how it was in those days. I must go back to the hospital wards.

I joined the ranks of the Red Cross and was sent, as an auxiliary nurse, to the large and formidable St. James's hospital in Leeds— Jimmy's as it was sometimes called. Here I worked in the maternity unit, sometimes on night duty, or in the chronic ward among the elderly and dying, in male and female wards, kitchens and sluice-rooms while living in the nurses' quarters.

Now I will add to my escutcheon a red cross on a white background, to remind me of those years of war in Britain.

Letters from India were few and far-between, and reached us with difficulty and delays. But I learned that Basil had sailed on one ship all round the coast of South Africa to Durban, where he had stayed a while before boarding the 'Ile de France', bound for Bombay. We eventually learned that he had arrived in Assam in north-east India, and started work in the Mizo Hills, southeast of Calcutta. At least I knew that he was safely there and among friends, though the hills were rather close to the volatile Burma border.

After a couple of years my father was appointed to a church in Great Malvern, and, not wishing to be left in Leeds on my own, I applied for a transfer to the Midlands. I was sent to a Worcester hospital, Ronkswood, which had been set up solely to receive war casualties.

I loved Malvern, with its rolling hills and lush green countryside. On my days off I cycled round the lanes on my stepmother's bike. In summer, one could buy cherries and plums at the wayside, and I would fill the basket on the handlebars and eat them as I went. At that time of the year the gutters of the town were full of discarded fruit stones.

The area was teeming with members of the forces. The secret Radar establishment was situated nearby, as well as a Royal Navy training camp and a large contingent of American soldiers, who roamed the streets and hills eager to pick up any female company they could. Even an American army chaplain, invited to the Manse for Sunday lunch, tried to make love to me on the couch in the front room. Although I avoided any involvement, I felt a little flattered until my stepmother told me that he had tried the same thing on with her! The whole place seemed to be full of Lost Boys, and we treated them as they came in from the fighting. It was hard to keep track of what was really happening in the war, but at last it seemed as if the tide was beginning to turn in favour of Britain and the Allies.

One morning there was a notice telling me that a passage was available for me to travel to India to join Basil. It was about mid-December 1944. Like him I had only a few days to get ready. I needed to try to get more coupons for clothes, pack my belongings, and arrange the journey north, since I was sailing from Glasgow.

Matron was inclined to refuse my resignation and block my exit, but I bluffed loudly, saying that the Government had to sanction my passage overseas, and, since it had done so, I must have every right to take it.

At last I was ready and my nursing friends came to wave me off from Worcester station. I was on my way to what could be my biggest adventure so far. In Glasgow all passengers were gathered secretly at an encampment of Nissen huts where we bedded for the night before being taken to the dockside. Once on board we found that our ship was the 'Batory', a Polish vessel that was taking army personnel to the war-front in Burma. The ship's ballroom had been turned into sleeping quarters, packed with bunks. We travelled over Christmas through the Mediterranean, and in Port Said, where we could go ashore, we bought oranges and saw lights brightening the night sky for the first time in more than four years of blackout.

I don't remember who, if anyone, met me in Bombay, but arrangements must have been made. I went with some shipboard friends to have an ice cream in one of the most luxurious hotels of the East, the Taj Mahal Hotel, just to celebrate life free from rationing and war conditions. In the evening I had to catch the Calcutta train on which I would spend the next three nights. I found that I was sharing a four-bunk carriage with a lady and two children. There was no corridor on the train, but dining-car attendants ran along the platform at one station to take our orders, and delivered the food when the train stopped further down the line. At night, lying on our bunks, we were often woken as we reached a station, and there were flashing lights and a bedlam of noises, slamming carriage doors, shouting porters and street vendors banging on windows even in the early hours of the morning.

As we drew near to our destination on the morning of the third day, I took my turn in the tiny bathroom to wash as well as I could, don my prettiest dress, and try to look my best after such a journey. Then I stepped out onto Calcutta station, and there was Bas.

Five

Mizoram

B ASIL had acquired practical skills and know-how during his time in India. He had visited Calcutta on more than one occasion to buy school equipment and bathroom furniture for the Mission, and transported it successfully to Aizawl, the main town in the Mizo hills for which we were heading. So he dealt authoritatively with my luggage, before steering me onto the streets of Calcutta.

After the restrictions of war-time Britain, Calcutta was a seething, teeming scene of human activity. Here were taxis driven by turbaned Sikhs, rickshaw men peddling their cycles, buses which were not only crammed inside but bore scores of white-robed figures clinging to the outside and riding on the roof. There were ragged beggars and homeless families camped on the pavements, alongside some of the most sumptuous shops one could find anywhere, and crowds pushed and jostled along every street.

I realise now that Basil must have planned our reunion with care. He wanted everything to enchant me, and it did. Somehow he had become friendly with the Swiss Ambassador and his wife, M. et Mme Fleury, who had invited us to dinner at the embassy that night. I think it may have been Twelfth Night, Epiphany, which in many parts of Europe is a time of great celebration and present-giving. I had left the U.K. about a week before Christmas, and the journey from Glasgow to Bombay would have taken three weeks. So we sat down to dinner with our very charming hosts, and after the main course, the lights were dimmed and the bearer came in carrying a Christmas pudding, wrapped in flames from burning brandy.

The following day we travelled to Silchar, on the border of what is now Bangladesh, and from which we could set out by jeep into the Mizo Hills. In Silchar, we were to spend a night with Merfyn Jones who had been one of the five Welshmen at Kingsmead College. Sleeping in bed in the Mission bungalow, at midnight we were startled abruptly into wakefulness by a weird howling just outside our window, like the wail of a banshee or a lost soul in torment. I clutched at Bas and gasped, "What is it?" By way of answer there was a rap on the door and Merfyn's voice called to us: "Don't worry, it's just a jackal. We get them now and then. It'll go away soon".

Basil had also made a friend of Colonel Williams who was in charge of the Assam Rifles in Aizawl. Education in Mizoram was Basil's remit, with the grand title of Honorary Inspector of Schools for the Mizo Hills. As part of his duties he had helped to set up a school for the children of the Gurkha soldiers stationed there. So we travelled the single road up into the hills in a Gurkha-driven army jeep. Such a vehicle was necessary in that terrain. Though the army had improved the road up into the hills, it was not surfaced but dug out of the steep, jungle-clad hillside. In the monsoon period of heavy rains throughout the summer months, it could be a perilous journey through mud, with a very steep drop on one side, all the way to Aizawl and beyond. Now we were travelling during the pleasantest season, the dry, cool time, when no rain fell, but the hillside drop was still there.

Nowadays, many years later, you can reach Aizawl by plane, but it must have been difficult to find or make a large level space for an airport. The whole country, about the size of Wales, is a series of hills and deep valleys. Many of the peaks are more than the height of Snowdon, and jungle growth covers all the slopes. Aizawl itself is about 4,000 feet above sea level, and from it, one can look out over five or six mountain ranges, each growing fainter as they stretch into the distance. When as often happens in the early morning, the valleys between the ridges are filled with cloud, the mountains look as if they are painted on the sky.

The first day's journey brought us to a halfway stop where we were to spend the first night in an army bungalow. When we arrived at twilight, I saw a fairly large building constructed, like all Mizo houses, out of wood and bamboo, and thatched with sun-grass. The bamboo was fresh and new, and before us was a pale, basket-work house standing on tall stilts above the forest floor. A flight of steps led up to the door and soft lamplight glowed in the unglazed windows.

Colonel Williams had left instructions for Indian servants to look after us. Basil had by then gained a working knowledge of the Mizo language, but he spoke only a few words of Hindi. As we entered through the door, we were met by three smiling men who bowed silently, hands together in greeting. When we were seated at the table, they brought dishes and drinks, more lamps and basins of water, flitting in and out, swiftly and wordlessly on bare feet like the spirit-servants who waited on Psyche in the house of Cupid, or Beauty in the home of the Beast.

When we had finished, they cleared the dishes and quietly melted away. We retired to the adjacent room and lay on the big bed with the lamp turned low. Surrounded by the white mist of the mosquito net we listened to the jungle rustlings below us, and the whooping of the how-huk monkeys as they swung among the trees. Full marks

Mizo girl carrying water in hollow
bamboo pipes (MDJ, 1951).

to Basil! I could not have had a more romantic introduction to Mizoram. In those days, the area was known as the Lushai Hills, the people as Lushais, and its chief town as Aijal; but for the purpose of this narrative, it will be less confusing if I keep throughout to the modern terms, Mizoram, the Mizos, and Aizawl.

We reached Aizawl the next day and the district of Mission Veng at its southern end, where we were to occupy a bungalow which crowned a hill beside the road, and was always referred to as the 'top bungalow'. Below us, a little further down the slope, was another bungalow occupied by two lady missionaries who quickly became great friends, Miss Gwen Rees Roberts and the older, comfortably-built Miss Katie Hughes. In the Mizo language they were known as Pi Teii (the small lady) and Pi Zaii (the singing lady) respectively. Pi Zaii was so called because she had a rich soprano voice, and had taught the Mizos, who took to Western music as if born to it and rivalled the Welsh with their singing. She had trained a choir and they had travelled across Northern India and sung to wide acclaim with a repertoire that included the Halleluiah chorus from Handel's Messiah. These two ladies were responsible for Sunday-school work and for the running of the Girls' School, which was built just below their bungalow. The Boys' Middle School was on a hill opposite our own on the other side of the road that ran south through the town. Also on that side were two more missionaries. Samuel Davies, with his wife and little daughter, was a comparatively old hand, but Meirion Lloyd, another of the Kingsmead students, had only recently arrived.

Our bungalow, like the rest, was made largely of asbestos, with a corrugated iron roof. It had two large bedrooms with dressing rooms and bathrooms, but no running water. There was a dining room and a newly added sitting room and a study for Bas. The kitchen, as in all the houses, was separate from the living quarters and it had an earthen floor and a black, wood-burning stove. We had three men-servants, a cook, a bearer, and a pani-wallah to fetch wood and water. At home, people raised their eyebrows at the mention of so many servants, but they themselves had electricity, tap water and gas as their menials, not to mention fridges and washing machines. Our food was kept in a sort of airy cabinet, which stood with each of its four feet in a tin of water to prevent the ubiquitous ants from climbing up and invading the larder. All cooking was done over the wood fire, and wood, our only fuel, had to be collected daily from the jungle around us. Water too had to be carried up from the streams which were at the bottom of the deep valleys and which often dried up in the rainless period.

In Mizo households it was usually the women and girls who performed the arduous task of water carrying. They bore hollow bamboo pipes, stacked in bamboo baskets, which they carried on their backs, supported on the shoulders and by a band across the forehead. In our bungalow compound there was a small tank, fed by a large one on the opposite hill that belonged to the government. But we were rationed during the dry season, and the pani-wallah had to carry water in the usual way from the streams.

In early summer, the drought would be suddenly broken by violent, lightning-flashing storms, when the rain pounded thunderously on our tin roof so that we had to shout to be heard above it. Then we all rushed into the compound with any vessel we could find; empty petrol tins, zinc baths—anything to catch the precious water. Shortly afterwards, the monsoon winds would bring the hot, wet season, when we had too much of it, all summer.

The dry season was the best and coolest time for going on tour, visiting the outlying villages where Basil was perhaps organizing the building of new schools. Soon after I arrived, I went with him, riding on one of the mission ponies, a new experience for me. I found it somewhat unnerving at first, because the animal insisted on walking right at the edge of the path and, looking over the side, I could see no ground beneath us but a long, long drop into green, jungly depths below.

The Mizos had their own system of agriculture. They kept very few animals, except chickens and pigs that were always around a village. We Europeans ate mostly poultry—skinny chickens bought live in the market. We were always suspicious of pork, not knowing what the animals had been eating themselves. Vegetables were plentiful, grown locally, and the main food was rice. Every spring, before the rains came, each village or group of villages would mark out a portion of the hillside, cut down the trees and scythe the undergrowth before setting fire to it. All was reduced to ashes, which fertilized the dug soil when the rains came. Then the rice was planted on the slopes. Thus, at that time of the year one might see whole hillsides in flames, and the smoke would drift over the valleys. It was called 'jhuming', and was in many ways a wasteful method of agriculture, but it was one that had been used for countless years. Sometimes the fires got out of hand at this season when everything was tinder dry.

I remember going on tour with Bas during jhuming time and at one point we found our way barred by an out-of-control fire. For about a quarter of a mile, both sides of the path leading to the village that we had to reach were lapped with flames and smoke hung in the air above. The village people would be waiting for us expecting our arrival, and the detour to avoid the fire would not allow us to reach them before nightfall. Certainly the horses would not go through such a flaming landscape, but Basil thought he and I could make it, if I was willing. So the horses and all the people carrying our baggage in bamboo baskets on their backs went around the long way. Bas grabbed my hand and we ran along a path about a yard wide, between two far-reaching expanses above and below us, of crackling, flaming ground. Jumping over the odd red-hot branch or stick that lay in our way, we emerged panting and triumphant, at a cooler, greener stretch of road.

Outside the village, the elders were waiting for us in a respectful row, and our way was lined on both sides by the boy scouts, saluting. Drums beat and a choir struck up a welcoming song. The British Royal Family could not have been more honourably received. A kettle was boiling on a roadside stove, and we were offered hot tea, sweetened with homegrown molasses in enamel mugs. The rest of our company, with the horses, did not arrive until much later.

3‌

During his time in Mizoram, Basil established more than a hundred primary schools in the villages, and appointed their first teachers. He was also responsible for Middle Schools, and a High School in Aizawl, and set up a Teacher Training College on the slope below our bungalow.

Every Mizo village wanted a school and a teacher, and deputations arrived regularly at our bungalow to put a petition before Pu Zawna as Basil was called. He always refused the presents they brought and stressed that such gifts would make no difference to his decision. But they were not so easily put off, and after they had gone, we found live chickens in little bamboo cages left at the kitchen door, or a bleating goat tied to the gate-post. The goats would eventually be eaten, but once, Bas, and Khuma, our bearer, decided that a larger than usual animal might do something for its keep. They shut themselves, with the goat, in an outside shed (called a 'go-down') and attempted to milk it. For some considerable time, the rest of us stood outside and listened enthralled to the shouting, bleating, thumping and wall-banging coming from the building. Eventually Bas and Khuma emerged looking hot and defeated. The nanny had objected violently to such indignities, and refused to cooperate. They had got about half a cupful out of her, and that she had kicked over!

I had been in Aizawl about a month when, one Sunday morning I fainted during a church service. I was brought round and taken gently outside to sit in a cooler spot, surrounded by a group of kindly, sympathetic Mizo ladies. "It's just the heat", I said apologetically, but they smiled indulgently at me and knowingly amongst themselves. They knew perfectly well what was happening, and I soon came to realise it myself. I was pregnant.

So the touring stopped, and all through the long sultry summer, I grew bigger and bigger. I had almost non-stop 'morning sickness' at first, and was much plagued with horse-fly bites on my legs. I was never attacked by a leech or by malaria-carrying mosquitoes, but the big horseflies would follow the animals. I got badly bitten and the bites went septic and troubled me all summer.

The baby was due about mid-November, and I would have to travel to the Mission hospital in Durtlang, about eight miles away, where Dr Gwyneth Roberts (Pi Puii, or Big Lady) held sway, with the assistance of Nurse Gwladys Evans (Pi Hruaii). I could not walk in my condition on the steep uphill path to Durtlang, nor would riding be a safe mode of transport. So a litter was made for me and four wiry Mizos carried me all the way, with Basil accompanying us on foot. The whole hillside around Durtlang was bright with blazing orange, not this time flames of fire, but flowers of the kind we call French marigolds which grow there in wild profusion.

Nowadays, whenever I see the frequent television scenes of women in labour, I am amused at the way they are overplayed. The actress screams and shouts as though someone had lit hell-fire under her. I do not remember it like that in all the times I have been in that situation and I should like to reassure prospective mothers that it is not necessarily so. I gloried in the effort, and gave it all I'd got. And I never found that I needed to scream and shout at the top of my voice. I had a little rhyme in my head, I don't know where it came from, but I got through each spell of contractions by singing or reciting it as fast as I could, to the tune of 'Frere Jacques', seeing how many times I could repeat it before the contraction ended.

> "Shakespeare, Milton, Shakespeare, Milton
> Shelley as well, Shelley as well,
> Ella Wheeler Wilcox, Ella Wheeler Wilcox,
> Ethel M. Dell, Ethel M. Dell".

I offer it as a tip to any woman in labour; it worked for me, anyway.

Gareth Ewart was born, a healthy and perfect eight-and-a-half pounds, at mid-day on 17th November, 1945. Like myself, he had made his first appearance just after the ending of a world war, for in Europe the conflict was over and the peace was signed. He grew apace, and took his first tottering but determined steps when he was ten months old. But I have never heard of a child so accident-prone.

His guardian angel certainly drew the short straw when the jobs were handed out.

We had bought a perambulator, left by some previous missionary. It was of the old type, high up on springs and large wheels, and big enough to accommodate quintuplets; not like the modern box on wheels. I strapped young Gareth into it one morning, and left it with brake clamped on the bungalow verandah. He jigged up and down in it until he had shifted the pram right to the edge, so that it fell the two or three feet down onto the grass below, with him inside. The pani-wallah one day left open the roof of the water tank long enough for the over-active child to fall in and have to be fished out before he drowned. On another occasion he tried to make friends with the horse grazing the compound, but Ginger was a somewhat short-tempered animal who lived up to his name. Gareth got bitten on the forehead and bears the scar to this day. The worst hazard was when he found the go-down door left open and went in to take a drink from the tin of kerosene inside. That really frightened me; I thought he was going to choke to death!

All our bath water had to be heated over the wood stove in the kitchen in a large kerosene tin, and Khuma had just taken a canful off the fire and set it on the floor when young Gareth came tearing in and fell over it, putting both his hands into the near-boiling water. It was not generally taught in those days that the best thing for scalds and burns was to immerse the affected part in cool water, and our hospital and doctor were a day's journey away in Durtlang. I nursed the poor mite as best I could in my bed, until a message reached Gwladys Evans and she arrived next morning and tended the poor blistered hands.

But that overworked guardian angel did a sterling job, and Gareth survived everything, and even thrived. Before he was a year old, I was once more pregnant, and his first sibling was on the way.

Every five years, missionaries were given a year in the U.K. It was called a 'furlough', and Bas was due for his. Dr Gwyneth was already taking hers, and was absent from the hospital in Durtlang. It was decided, therefore, that we would travel to Shillong, in the Khasi Hills of North Assam, so that I could give birth to our next child in the big mission hospital there, under the care of Dr Arthur Hughes. Then we would go on from there to Calcutta and Bombay to catch the ship for the U.K. and Wales.

I was pretty near my time when we faced the three to four-day journey to North Assam, and it was decided that we would travel, not by road along the bumpy, muddy track in monsoon time, but by riverboat to the plains. We had to take a half-day truck ride down to Sairang on the river, and there, with Khuma and our entire luggage, including the big pram with Gareth sleeping in it, we settled into three long boats.

There were two sets of rapids to negotiate, with frenzied shouting and plying of paddles from the boatmen. Reaching the plains we disembarked at a railway line. There were tracks but no platform, and no shelter from the heat of the sun. We waited a long time before a train arrived and then I had to be hoisted up about four feet into the carriage. The compartments were all crowded and Khuma had to travel in the one behind us. He left it at the first stop and came running to join us, followed by angry shouts and gestures from other travellers. Nowadays, the Mizo people are proud to class themselves as an important part of Mother India. In those days, on the very eve of her independence from British rule, the country was riven with divisions among many different languages, faiths and cultures, and there was little love lost between the hill people and those of the plains. Tempers and quarrels flared up easily.

After a night in Sylhet at the northern end of the plains, we travelled for a full day by hired car up into the cooler Khasi Hills, to Shillong, where a Mission building was at our disposal, and Welsh friends came to greet us. Dr Arthur Hughes gave me a quick examination and declared that I was very lucky the child had not made its entry into the world during the journey!

This child was in no hurry! We had our passage booked on a ship from Bombay, but days passed and still the infant showed no inclination to come out and get on with the business of living. In the end, fearful of time slipping by, it was decided to induce the birth, and Peter Hugh was born on the fourth day of August 1947. Just over a week later, on the day I left the hospital with him, there was singing and dancing in all the streets as India celebrated its independence and the end of the British Raj.

Our troubles and delays were not yet over. I had been back in the Khasi bungalow only a few days when Basil fell ill and Arthur Hughes diagnosed diphtheria. He had to be isolated immediately, and our passage to Britain was cancelled until a later date.

Poor Khuma was anxious to go back to his wife and family in Mizoram, and did not feel he could linger any longer in Shillong. So I reluctantly said 'Damtakin' (goodbye) to him. One of our missionary friends found a little Khasi lady who was willing to shop and cook for me each day. I could speak no Khasi and she no English, but we managed somehow. I felt not a little lost with two babies in an alien land and Basil unreachable in the isolation ward. We came through it all with the help of friends. Eventually, Bas came out of hospital none the worse, and we booked a new passage home and faced the long journey to Calcutta and across northern India to Bombay. I recall lying on my bunk in a train steaming through North Assam with Peter at my breast. We were sharing a four-bunk compartment with two British soldiers going home. In the early morning, one of them raised the blinds, and looking out of the carriage window I saw, stretching along the horizon, the majestic snow-clad peaks of the Himalayas, tinged with rosy light in the sunrise.

Peter was none the worse for the travelling, so long as he could connect up to the milk-bar on demand, and adventurous little Gareth got his fill of excitement. He could always be spotted among a sea of dark heads because he had a shock of flaxen hair which he kept into adulthood. A friend in charge of the London Missionary Society mission centre in Calcutta where we stayed patted his white locks and said, "You ought to call him Kanchenjunga". "No", I said, "Neverest would be nearer the mark!"

Indian independence was not only a matter for rejoicing, it brought with it a flaring of hostilities between Muslims and Hindus, with some dreadful incidents of slaughter and suffering. Arriving at Calcutta station we had to pick our way through crowds of refugees, camped out in the wide covered entrance.

With our little family we made the train journey across India, and caught the boat from Bombay. Eighteen days later we landed in Liverpool.

Six

Wales and India

FURLOUGH was not really a time for rest. Basil had quite a full schedule of travel and meetings around Wales, and I took a few appointments myself, speaking about the work of the Mission. We spent the whole year staying with either his parents in Penrhiwceiber, or my own in Bangor, for my father was now Old Testament Professor at Bangor University College, and lived in a house on the Menai Straits.

It takes a good many years, I find, before the umbilical cord to our original family is finally cut. My own children in later years treated our establishment as 'home' long after they had left it. I was thankful for it, such assumptions are both the cause and outcome of precious family bonding. In 1947, neither of our families complained, though our presence must have been an inconvenience, to say the least, with night-crying babies and washing lines full of nappies every day. So, wipe your eyes you mothers grieving over the lad's departure from the nest. Without any doubt, he will be back with washing, hearty appetite, girlfriends and, before long, a family. The final severance will not come until you are quite ready for it!

The year slipped away almost unnoticed, and soon we were preparing for our return to Mizoram, this time leaving from Southampton. A few days after embarking, somewhere in the Mediterranean, I fell ill. I was feverish and had to retire to the cabin in the afternoon, with Peter sleeping beside me. Bas had the task of looking after Gareth on deck, but it was not long before they joined us. Gareth was dripping wet and pools formed on the cabin floor. It seemed he had fallen in the deep end of the swimming pool when his father was not looking, and had to be fished out. The guardian angel on this occasion was in the form of a teenage boy, to whom we owed much.

My fever turned out to be mumps, which I must have picked up on the mainland before we left Britain. Gareth also soon showed all the symptoms. The pair of us and Peter, who needed my care, were packed off to the sick bay with our swollen faces for the rest of the voyage. When we landed in Bombay, we feared that further travel might be restricted for us, but mumps in those days was not classed as at all serious, just one of those childish lapses which it was good to have had and left behind you. We went straight onto the Calcutta train and were almost recovered by the time we reached Silchar. However, in Silchar, Peter showed obvious signs of the disease, and later we learned that Merfyn Jones's bearer, who petted and dandled him on his lap, had paid for his kindness by contracting mumps too. One wonders how far it spread after that!

We settled back into life in the top bungalow in Aizawl, and when Gareth was about five years old I decided to start lessons with him. He could have attended the Mizo boys' school; both boys had picked up the language, along with English, for they had many little friends among the local children. But the time would come, all too soon when they must fit into a U.K. education system, and I was the only one who could prepare them for that, untrained amateur that I was.

I was determined that it should be, as far as possible, like a proper school with a classroom and a timetable, even at so young an age. So I turned the dressing-room next to their bedroom into a schoolroom, and managed to get a small blackboard and easel made. I taught both boys to read, mainly by making a large number of small picture cards for every simple noun or verb with matching cards of words, and we played all sorts of games with them. They both quickly picked up reading skills, and many other lessons grew from that. We had stories and talks about British birds and animals and plants and, of course, numbers and simple arithmetic.

A Salvation Army missionary couple came to live in Aizawl. They had a son, John, a few years older than Gareth, and they asked if I would accept him into the 'school'. We got along fine, in spite of the age difference. I remember that we even had a prize-giving day when we invited all our friends and put on a show, a performance of the Mad Hatter's Tea-Party from *Alice in Wonderland*. Peter was too young for a big speaking part, but he made an excellent dormouse. Gareth was the March Hare, John the Mad Hatter and I, the only 'girl' played Alice. The performance was much appreciated.

Peter was four-and-a-half and Gareth was six when Elaine was born in Durtlang in the first hour of the first day of the second half of the century. Now we had a little daughter. The Mizos gave their own language names to all the missionaries' children. Gareth was known as Zoduha, 'Beloved of Mizoram', Peter as Zochuana, 'Pride of Mizoram', and Elaine was called Lalpari, 'Flower of the Lord'. Pu is the title for Mr and Pi for Mrs, so Basil and I were Pu Zawna and Pi Zawni. But it was the custom as soon as a son was born to call the mother by his name, so I had become Zoduha nu.

I had of course been having lessons in the Mizotawng language from the start, and I could speak it enough to communicate with the servants and to understand the gist of conversation. However, I never became fluent in it as Basil did, or for that matter, the

Mizo mother and baby (MDJ, 1951).

children, who seemed to pick it up from friends with no trouble at all. It was a fairly simple language, written down in Roman script with phonetic spelling and none of the exceptions and complications of English. But, like Chinese, it was tonal. The same words, uttered in a high or low, a rising or a falling tone, could mean something quite different. So speaking it in the almost musical cadences which the Mizos themselves used was very difficult, and I never really mastered the skill.

The children all thrived. I fed each of them at the breast for six months at least. There was little choice for I never saw a feeding bottle or a packet of baby-food in all the time we were in Mizoram. The Mizo mothers carried their babies with them all day, and had no cradles or prams. The infants were bound to their mother's back with the 'puan', as the Mizo all-purpose cloth was called. Men and women both wore it round the waist and over the shoulder. It was woven from cotton grown in the jhum, and decorated with traditional patterns in bright colours.

The common childish diseases did not pass us by—all three children caught measles. I can see Elaine now, at about two years old, lying naked on the bed covered with red spots. One summer all of them caught whooping-cough, which lasted for months and would not go until the dryer weather came.

We employed an 'ayah' whose name was Hliri, who washed the nappies and looked after Elaine while I was teaching the boys. I was sometimes able to help with Mission work, but I did not go on tour again.

We Europeans sometimes held parties to celebrate anniversaries or special occasions. I organised more than one in the top bungalow. The Governor of Mizoram in the last days of the British Raj was a Scotsman called Ranald MacDonald, who, with his wife Daphne, gave a Christmas party in Government House, to which we were all invited. Gareth was very small and I took him along in the big pram. He slept soundly in it while, in the adjoining room a few yards away, we danced Scottish reels to the accompaniment of bagpipes played by a magnificent band of Gurkha soldiers in turbans and tartan kilts.

Once President Nehru came to Aizawl and we all met and shook hands with him, I being very large and pregnant at the time.

From time to time, our household was enriched by a present of livestock. We were once given a toucan, a black and white bird with an outsize yellow beak. The Mizo name was 'haia', so Haia he became. He needed no cage but would sit on the edge of the mantelpiece, in a particular spot, while we tossed pieces of orange or banana and watched him deftly catch them. When we moved into an adjacent room, he would swoop gracefully through the door and alight on the 'almira' (Hindi word for a wardrobe) and spend the night with us. If we went for a walk to church or to the bazaar, he would accompany us, flying from tree to tree, waiting until we came out, ready for the return journey. Then came a time when he began to go on jaunts without us, but he would always come back to his perch on the mantelpiece at sundown. One day, probably in the mating season, he found a good reason to stay away and we saw him no more. We all felt sad because he had become one of the family and we missed him, but he had a right to make his own family and live in his own way.

Someone else gave us two beautiful white rabbits that wandered about the house and compound, and a little later we received a tiny wild civet cat. He was an enchanting bundle of fur, but he grew! Soon he learned to growl most alarmingly, spitting and displaying his undoubted wild nature. One day we found both the white rabbits slaughtered rather gruesomely, so he had to be taken back to the jungle and released. I'm sure he could well look after himself!

The monsoons would bring cicadas, chirruping loudly all evening and praying mantis insects on the wall with their little 'hands' together. One summer a swarm of bees decided to settle in a low cupboard in the boys' bedroom. They were quite orderly, going in and out all day about their business, but I was always afraid the children might get stung. Basil asked for help from the headmaster of the Boys' School, who was a skilled apiarist. He came round and spent a whole day lying on his back, half inside the cupboard without any protective clothing and with insects crawling all over him, while slowly and patiently he poked his stick through the swarm to find their queen. Reaching her at last, he carried her outside to a tree on the edge of the compound, with all her loyal subjects following behind in a dark cloud. As far as I knew he sustained no sting throughout the whole operation. There's skill and patience for you!

We did occasionally meet snakes, but only rarely. Young Gareth used to like going round barefoot, like his Mizo friends. I was afraid of ants and leeches and other nasty creatures and told him to wear his shoes. One day he left the lunch table to join his waiting pals and, after he had gone, I found his footwear under the chair where he had kicked them off. Surprisingly he turned up a little later looking for them and he seemed somewhat upset. I asked him why and, backed up by his friends, in a mixture of Mizotawng and English, he told me that a snake had slithered across his bare feet. Thanks to his angel he had had the sense to keep perfectly still until it had gone. The small ones were often the most poisonous.

In the bathroom next to the dressing room that we had turned into a baby-bedroom, there was an outlet pipe in the floor. Our bath had to be filled by hand and the water was afterwards tipped away into the garden down this pipe. Snakes liked to come up it too, and I once found one behind the baby's cot—thankfully no baby in it at the time! After that we were careful to stop up the pipe when it was not in use.

In the middle of all these duties and diversions, the Muse was refusing to lie down and be quiet. While we were still on furlough, he had begun to nudge me, and I had a few attempts at painting landscapes. I was itching to take up a pencil or a brush and get involved in the fascinating business of making pictures. No-one had recorded the country of Mizoram or its people in paint; here around me was untouched subject matter. Art materials could not, of course, be found in the bazaars of Aizawl, and would have been difficult to order by post from Calcutta, but I had brought back with me from Britain, pencils and paper, brushes and water-colour paints, and even some oil paints and a couple of canvases. The oil materials lay waiting for a long time, but I did a lot of pencil sketching, mainly of figures.

The Mizo people made excellent subjects, and I would sketch them at every opportunity: Khuma and others of the household, mothers with babies, old ladies or young boys and girls standing stock still, so patiently for me, in water-carrying mode with a basket of bamboo pipes on their backs. They exclaimed in wondering delight when I showed them a recognizable portrait and they could name the sitter. One courteous family allowed me to sit all day in a corner of their one-room house, painting them as they went about their business around the hearth. Alas I have very few of those drawings now, they all seem to have disappeared. Only one water-colour of Mizo houses below our bungalow hangs now on the wall of my bedroom.

My love of drama and theatre had always made me interested in another form of art, puppets. To produce a play you need the help of a lot of other people, but a puppet-play could be a solo affair. Besides, it gave one scope for theatrical design. While nursing during the war years I spent a lot of my time, when free from work on the wards, making a set of 'Punch and Judy' figures out of papier maché, brightly painted and with clothes of brilliant colours. On returning to Mizoram after furlough, I packed these dolls and took them with me; they would amuse the boys at any rate. Back in Aizawl, I got a carpenter to make me the frame for a theatre, which I draped with a colourful Mizo 'puan'. I made a proscenium and scenery and gave a performance or two to the open-mouthed astonishment of the Mizos, who were not sure if they were supposed to laugh or not. They were much too considerate to laugh if it was not meant to be humorous.

Punch may seem a much too English character to be accepted out East, but the Mizos, as my language pundit told me, had a similar amoral rogue in their old folk tales. He was called, if I remember rightly, Chura-bura, and I was told a tale of how he got the better of a tricksy devil woman. My teacher helped me to write a script of the story in Mizotawng, and I made two new puppets to include that play in my repertoire.

It happened that about that time, India's Minister for Home Affairs was making an official visit to Mizoram. A concert was planned in his honour, and I was asked to perform with my puppets as one of the items. I did both shows, 'Punch and Judy' in English, and 'Chura-bura' in Mizotawng. When I was introduced to him afterwards, the Minister wondered, with a mischievous smile, if I manipulated my husband as adroitly as I did the puppets!

We spent that following Christmas in Durtlang, so it must have been the week before Elaine was born and I was 'in waiting'. On Christmas Day I took my puppet theatre to the hospital wards, and then to the segregated T.B. patients, and put my dolls through their paces again. The children especially enjoyed it, though I'm sure they were convinced the Pi was completely mad!

Basil was busy with a group of Mizos translating parts of the Old Testament into their language. The New Testament had been in print for some time, but the Old had not been completed. As his second five-year term drew to an end he told me that he thought we would not be returning to India after this next furlough. It was increasingly apparent that the Mizo people were more than capable of looking after their own affairs, educational and ecclesiastical. They did not need us, although the welcome they gave us was as warm as ever.

Basil's decision undoubtedly had something to do with the fact that the boys, at any rate, would not return; they must attend school in the U.K. Gareth was eight and Peter six and we would have had to place them in boarding school and the care of relatives. I deeply hated the idea of being parted from them in that way, but I would have stayed with Bas and left them behind if he had so decided.

So I welcomed his decision with heartfelt relief, but with some sorrow too. Leaving Mizoram was an undoubted wrench, we had many close friends there. They are a people of great charm. Only half a century before, they had been a race of headhunting warriors, ruled by tribal rivalries and by belief in evil spirits in the natural world around them. After the advent of the first missionaries, the whole country had embraced Christianity, and they were a peaceful, law-abiding society, avid for education.

I once visited the only jail in all Mizoram with Basil. It was an open compound in Aizawl, where a few mild-mannered men were housed in bamboo huts, with nothing resembling bars. They sang hymns with us and I could not imagine that any of them had committed anything very dreadful. Western societies, with violence and anti-social behaviour on the increase, might learn a lot from these mature, courteous people.

The day came when we said our 'goodbyes' and I was able to speak my thanks and farewells to the assembled church gathering in Mizotawng. Foremost in my thoughts was regret for all the things I had not managed to do while living amongst them. Two lines of a hymn kept coming into my mind:

"Help me oppressed by things undone,
    O, thou whose deeds and dreams were one".

We left Mizoram with the words of another hymn ringing in our ears, as a great company sang resoundingly, "God be with you till we meet again".

I have been wondering what symbol of Mizoram I could include in my coat of arms, and I think it must be the bamboo. From that extraordinary plant they fashion their houses, furniture, baskets and containers, kitchen utensils and just about everything needed for domestic living. Parts of it can even be eaten, too. So I will have bamboo stems to remind me of the years we spent among them, a happy and rewarding time.

Yet, useful as the bamboo plant may be to the Mizo people, it can be their bane, because it is a major source of sustenance to their greatest pest—the rat. Thieving rats are responsible for the loss of a large portion of every household's rice store. The dominant type of bamboo in Mizoram is an extraordinary plant that has the peculiarity of flowering only once in every fifty years. All these bamboo are related and none will produce flowers in the years between. In the fiftieth year, they all flower together and produce large quantities of a fruit that attracts the rat population and swells their numbers considerably.

In the year following the flowering, the bamboo does not produce new shoots and as a result, the rats have to look elsewhere for food. They inevitably turn to the ripening rice crop in the jhums. It is said that a band of marauding rats can devour in one night, the harvest that was to have kept several villages alive that year. Thus every year following flowering is followed by a year of hardship and starvation for the villagers.

Such a phenomenon never took place while we were in Mizoram. The previous occasion had been in 1910, but after we had left the country in 1958, it happened again and 1959 was a year of deprivation. The hardship was a major factor in an uprising that followed. Discontented Mizos joined the Mizo National Front and carried on guerilla warfare against government forces for a number of years. With India's growing prosperity and technological advance, the rat problem may well be better controlled in the future in those years following bamboo flowering and I hope that the previous levels of suffering may be softened or averted with time.

It was not long before the authorities told all missionaries that, after they left on furlough, they would not be allowed back into the country. Gwen Rees Roberts, Pi Teii, had to give up the work that she had so faithfully and competently undertaken in the Girls' School. It was a number of years before the rebellion died down, and only after there had been a shoot-out between the rebels and the Assam Rifles in Mission Veng; mission buildings, including the top bungalow, sustained bullet damage. It was a time of great uncertainty and danger, and Gwen herself has written about it with much more authority than I can command, in a book entitled *Memories of Mizoram*, published in 2001.

Seven

Aberystwyth

IN 1954, air travel was still too expensive, and not the accepted norm that it is today. We had to make the long journey by train between Calcutta and Bombay, where we boarded a ship to Britain. It was December, and once again I was to have a Christmas on board.

In Calcutta, Bas and I had managed somehow to buy small presents with which to fill the children's stockings, and also bigger gifts for them. I recall a doll for Elaine. On Christmas morning we watched them open all their parcels in the cramped cabin. Then Basil took the three of them off to the dining-room while I did some clearing up before joining them later. I was making my way along one of the long white corridors of the ship, full of the warm feelings which that most exciting season of the year always rouses in me, especially enhanced on this occasion because we were going 'home'. In the passage-way I met a member of the crew, dark-skinned and black-haired, and, without thinking whether it was appropriate or not, I smiled broadly and wished him a "Happy Christmas'. He stopped in his tracks, turned and beckoned me to follow him, and I did. We went down and down into the bowels of the vessel, past the crew's sleeping quarters—rows of hammocks—until we reached a small room, which must have been a kind of common-room. There he stood back and gestured for me to look and I saw a table, surrounded by other dark faces, all watching me expectantly. On the table was a model, obviously of the Nativity scene. There was a small effigy of the Virgin and child at the centre, and other figures around them. I don't remember it clearly, but it was, you might say, a 'trashy' representation, yet it brought tears of emotion to my eyes.

"It's beautiful!" I said, "beautiful" and I meant it.

They all smiled at me and looked pleased. Then my guide took me back and I found my way to the breakfast table and told Bas all about it. I learned afterwards that most of the crew came from the West of India Province of Goa, which had been largely Christian-ised by the Catholic missionary, St Francis Xavier in the 16th Century. My life was, and would be, so very different from the life of that Indian sailor, that you would think we had no link between us. Yet we had in common the fact that we both knew and under-stood the real meaning of Christmas; and in that I was closer to him than to many of my countrymen.

Back in Wales we were not staying this time with long-suffering relatives. Sadly Basil's mother had died from a heart attack during his last period in India. The Mission had acquired the use of a large building in Llanfairfechan on the North Wales coast to accom-modate missionaries, home from the field, while they spent their furlough or settled their future lives. It was a sort of holiday home for a group of children in care, and was unoccupied for most of the year except for a housekeeper who was in residence. We settled into a part of it, temporarily, and the boys went to the local school for a couple of terms. It was only years later that Gareth told me that he and Peter were bullied, not only by the other pupils, but also by their teacher, because they spoke no Welsh. It was a poor intro-duction to school life for two small boys from a very different life abroad. I have heard of other children who were similarly treated because their language was Welsh in an English-speaking school. Such teachers do not deserve their positions, and should be sent back to college for further training!

One incident only stands out in my mind from the months we spent in that house in Llanfairfechan. Basil's father, Farv, now a widower, came to stay with us for a short holiday. One afternoon when Bas was away at a meeting and the boys in school, I had an unavoidable and much-needed appointment with the local dentist, and I asked Farv to look after three-year-old Elaine while I was out. When I returned he was sitting enjoying his pipe on a seat in the front garden. "Where's Elaine?" I asked with a sense of foreboding. In my experience 'baby-sitting' to a man meant just that, sitting, while the baby did whatever took its fancy. "Oh somewhere inside", said Farv vaguely, puffing contentedly. "The little girl from next door came round and they're playing". I opened the front door and was confronted with the sight of a waterfall cascading down the stairs. Rushing up to the orphanage-style bathroom I found it swimming in several inches of water. The room had a row of about eight washbasins against the opposite wall, each with hot and cold. The two little girls had put the plugs in every one of them and turned all the taps full on!

I screamed for Farv to come and help and began the almost impossible task of mopping up as hard as I could. The housekeeper was out for the afternoon, but I could hear the sound of running water coming from her sitting-room which was directly beneath the bathroom. When I flung open the door I saw it streaming through a wide crack in the ceiling plaster and splashing onto her table beneath. The two little girls were playing happily in the front room. When the housekeeper returned that evening I had to perform the biggest grovelling act of which I was capable. I don't blame her if she found it hard to forgive us, and I'm sure she breathed a sigh of relief when we finally departed.

That day came before the summer was out. Basil happened one day to spot an advertisement in a paper which he picked up on a train, for a lecturer in Religious Studies at the Education Department of the University College of Wales in Aberystwyth. He applied for the post and was jittery and unapproachable for the next few weeks. I never doubted for a moment that he would get the job. I could not see how any Board would be foolish enough to reject him; he was ideal for such a post, so it was no surprise to me when he announced that we were going to live in Aberystwyth.

The town and its environs were well-known to Bas from his College days, but I had never seen it before. Our immediate concern was to find a house; my stepmother obligingly offered to look after Elaine, and the two boys were sent to Basil's sister Rene, while we went on our search for suitable accommodation.

Starting from Bangor we travelled the latter part of the journey by bus to Aberystwyth, and I remember looking out of the windows as we passed through the village of Tre-Taliesin, my eyes reaching across the expanse of Cors Fochno to Borth and Cardigan Bay beyond. On a summer day, it was a view of enchantment, and I hugged myself as I thought, "This is where we'll live from now on!"

We found a cottage in Tre-Taliesin itself. It was small and had no bathroom. Indeed, there was no running water. There was a tap in the lane just outside the front gate, and previous inhabitants had used that as their nearest source of water. But we could afford the price that was being asked, and from the back bedroom window, we could look across a small garden and the expanse of bog-land beyond it to the sea. It was called 'Oak Villa',—a ridiculous English name, which we always intended to change, but never got round to.

We settled in and the family was reunited. The boys, and in time Elaine, went to the local school which was run by a charismatic headmaster, Hugh Evans. He welcomed them without reservation and became a good friend, so that they attended school without any trauma and began to enjoy being part of the community. We turned an upstairs room into a bathroom, and Basil, who loved making cement, did various alterations in the house and made a garage and approach out of the lean-to shed against the western wall. He bought his first car, a little Ford Popular, which did valiant service for a number of years. This was the cottage in the country that I had dreamed of in pre-marital days.

I was busy enough and found no time to satisfy the Muse, except with drama. We attended the Welsh-speaking chapel, 'Rehoboth' and one Christmas I produced a Nativity play with all available village children. A year later I was asked to arrange, with them, some entertainment for a big rally that the Mission Board was staging in Aberystwyth at the Parish Hall.

I wrote a version of 'Pilgrim's Progress', with children taking all the parts and a choir of adults singing between scenes to cement the whole together. Hugh Evans agreed to be Bunyan, the narrator, behind the curtain. It was a lot of work; I made all the costumes myself, including angels' wings, painted gold. But everyone, the choir, parents, the carpenter who made a great wooden cross for the scene when Christian loses his burden, and especially the children themselves, were wonderful. Peter played Christian and I was proud of him, as I was of them all. We played it first in the schoolroom of Rehoboth chapel, and the next day we had a bus to take us with all our props to the Parish Hall in Aberystwyth. One lady came to me afterwards and said, somewhat breathily, "That was the most beautiful thing I have ever seen!" You can't get higher praise than that!

But we left Taliesin after only four years. Gareth had started in the Grammar School in the town, and Basil was making the same journey to college each day. We felt it would be a good idea to be nearer their places of work. Besides, I was pregnant again and the cottage would be too small to accommodate another family member.

One of Basil's colleagues was leaving her family home on the outskirts of the town, a three-storey house with a small garden. It seemed ideal, and we moved in. Another son, Malcolm Rosser, was born a few months later, in the hospital that could be seen from the upper-storey windows of our new house, and I was busy, busy, busy!

Two years later I was busier still when another one made his appearance, Christopher Paul. Only then did I get a washing machine to help with the towelling nappies, which are rarely used nowadays. By the time Mark Alun came along, three years after that, Gareth and Peter were in college and Basil had worked for, and achieved, his PhD.

Life was full and, in these years, the only painting I had time for was slapping vinyl-silk on walls and gloss on window-frames. But when Mark began school, I found an opportunity for more puppet play. In one of the attic rooms, I made a fair-sized puppet theatre, with finger-puppets, which formed the cast of two plays, my beloved 'Hansel and Gretel' and a version of 'The Tailor of Gloucester' from a Beatrix Potter story. Dressed all in black, at the back of the stage and with strategic lighting, I could not be seen while I made the witch or the little mice dance on the ends of my fingers to the recorded sound track and music in the background.

With Malcolm and Elaine helping, I took the theatre to the Primary School in Aberystwyth and gave performances as an end-of-term Christmas treat. Some years later, I settled down to make a set of small figures, about fifteen inches high, with padded bodies and limbs, heads made of table-tennis balls, hands, feet and features formed with 'plastic wood'. I dressed them all in historical costumes, men, women and children, representing fashions in Britain from about 1450 to the Edwardian era.

Ever since the days when I took that Royal Drawing Society examination and drew the picture of the embarrassed 15th century jester, I had been interested in costume—historical costume that is. I was never a very natty dresser myself, and always envied women who could knot a scarf to look chic. I bought books on the subject to study it further and had enjoyable forays to the shops to find the right materials for the clothes. I dyed animal wool for hair and used feathers for decoration. Over a twelve-month period I completed forty-five dolls altogether, and was sometimes asked to show them and give talks, mainly at W.I. meetings. A television channel got to hear of them and a crew came to the house with their microphones and cameras to make a programme about them. When it was shown, we went next door to see it because they had colour television and ours was only black and white. What most took my eye was that I was shown on the screen, more than once, the wrong way round. I was working left-handed which I could not have been. I wonder now, every time I see a left-handed person on the box, whether it is really so or have they got the picture back-to-front? A decade later, when we left the house and moved to a smaller dwelling, I sold all the figures to the Ceredigion Museum in Aberystwyth, where they were on show in a glass case for more than twenty-five years.

Such activities could be indulged in while looking after small children, but composing and painting pictures required time to myself, without any diversions. As the younger boys grew and became involved in school and football and entertained themselves, I slipped back into drawing and painting. I decided to join the Cardiganshire Art Society, founded and headed by the late Hywel Harries who taught art in Ardwyn Grammar School. The Society had monthly meetings with guest speakers, and it also held an exhibition each year in the English Primary School in Aberystwyth. All members could enter several pictures if they wished.

I still had a vague idea that the only subject suitable for a picture that was to hang on somebody's wall was a landscape, and I went out into the countryside with my board and pencil and little folding stool. I'm ashamed to say that I have never learned to drive. I did get a learner's licence when we lived in Taliesin, but never completed the course before the three younger boys came along and took up my time and energy. But my husband was always ready to take me out, with my packet of sandwiches and a thermos, to any scene which had previously taken my fancy, and leave me there until he came and collected me before the family returned from school, hungry for an evening meal. The spots I chose were often remote, and I saw no-one all day. I liked the solitude and more than once danced wildly all by myself on a hill-top with no-one there to see.

I never took paints or brushes on such a jaunt, but made detailed and extensive drawings of trees and streams and hillsides with my pencil, all the while soaking up the colour and getting ideas for a painted version. That, I made at home on a table, putting a good deal of myself into the picture to produce the atmosphere I wanted.

But my real inclination was to illustrate stories of mystery and magic, of the kind that I so enjoyed picturing in my childhood days in the Sanctum at Handsworth. So I did some pictures of Welsh stories now and then, along with the landscapes, and I entered some of each kind in the Cardiganshire Art Society's annual exhibition. I found I could sell, which gave me a heady feeling. Moreover, I got requests for pictures privately, which was even more exciting.

Yet I was still such an amateur! I had not learned to stretch my paper before painting on it, and I had trouble with the way it buckled under water. My use of watercolour meant a brush full of very liquid paint, and it would run into the valleys and grooves made by the undulating paper. I soon found that I must prepare my surface before using it. Now I immerse the sheet of paper in water (usually the bath) shake off the bulk of the water, and lay the sheet on a piece of fibreboard. Then I wipe it gently with a piece of clean, dry cloth, stroking from the centre outwards, and tape all round the edge with brown sticky tape. When it is dry it is stretched tight, like the surface of a drum, because the paper has contracted. It will remain so, however liquid the paint I use.

I made my own frames, and, as in everything else, I was the amateur. I did not feel justified in paying the cost of having them made for me. This I felt was my hobby and it must pay for itself. More than that I wanted to make money, not a great deal, and not for myself, but enough to justify spending my time and energy on it instead of working for the family at home. Every penny I have earned on painting has gone directly into the family coffers and never into a personal fund for myself. I longed to be professional enough to bring in some rewards.

I made some kind of progress and it brought me more and more towards story illustrating rather than landscape. In 1974, I asked permission of the elders of the church that we attended, St David's in Bath Street, Aberystwyth, to hold a small exhibition in their schoolroom during one fortnight in the summer, and they kindly granted it. They had screens and I hung pictures on both sides of these, landscapes and folk-tale illustrations, all watercolours. Bas typed out copies of a programme for me and I sat in my seat each day watching people come and go, and making the occasional sale. I made no entry charge, but a collecting bowl and an invitation to contribute to Christian Aid funds placed at the entrance/exit did very well, especially on wet days when people came in from the rain.

So it was that a few years later I had sufficient courage to put in a similar request for a personal exhibition in the newly opened gallery of the Aberystwyth Arts Centre on Pen-glais Hill above the town. The authorities looked indulgently on my application and I found myself working to get together enough paintings for such an event. I gathered forty-five pictures, mostly new, but a few borrowed back from previous buyers. The exhibition was entitled 'Welsh Landscape and Legend' and it was just that.

Bas presented me with a book of Charles Rennie Macintosh watercolours as a celebration gift. In it he wrote, "To my darling Peggy, on the occasion of her first major exhibition, with much love, Bas, September 1979".

All of my subsequent career, I date from that exhibition, and I came away from the opening night almost as exultant as I had been after that Speech Day in T.H. so long before. Once again I was photographed for television; I think it was for a programme called 'Heddiw'. It was only a brief appearance, but it gave me valuable advertisement.

The most exciting and far-reaching result of all, was an approach by the newly founded Welsh Arts Council, now known as the Arts Council of Wales. This was to send them some samples of work, with a view to illustrating a new children's version of the Four Branches of the Mabinogi, being prepared for publication by Professor Gwyn Thomas, University of Wales, Bangor. Some members of the Arts Council had been to my exhibition and thought I might be what they were looking for.

My mind boggled! Not only was I being offered an illustrating commission, but for such a book! As far as I knew, the Welsh stories had never, up until that time, been fully illustrated in colour, and of all prizes it was the one I most desired; I could not believe my luck! It was not long before I signed a contract that fulfilled all the clichés about a dream come true.

All my life I have been an amateur. I never did get to take that teacher training course. I have done laundering, housekeeping, cookery, baby-rearing, gardening, frame-making, preaching, teaching and drama-directing, home decorating and dress-making; in every case floundering and experimenting, hit-or-miss, with no proper qualifications or training. As an artist, I was often asked, "Are you amateur or professional?" I have been on the verge of saying "Yes" to either.

One day, young Mark came home from school and said that he had been required to fill in a form, which left a space for parents' occupations.

"What should I have put for Dad, Mum?" he asked.

"Lecturer in the Education Department of U.C.W., Aberystwyth", I said, adding as an afterthought, "What did you put for me?"

I thought he would say, "Housewife", or even "Nothing", but he answered, without hesitation, "Free-lance artist and illustrator".

It made my day! No! It made my head-up outlook for the rest of my life! At the age of sixty I had somehow reached professional status in the career of my choice!

Wedding Day,
27th September 1941.

During my time as a
Red Cross nurse in 1942.

Basil's father and mother on our Wedding Day.

A post-wedding photograph of Basil and myself in 1941.

In Mizoram before 1947: Basil and colleagues in the Presbyterian
Mission District of Aizawl, before my arrival in 1945.

Boy Scout Rally outside the Boys' Middle School in the Mission District,
with Basil seated 8th from left, 2nd row.

At the Tennis Club, with Basil 9th from left, front row,
the children and myself on extreme right at the front.

Our family in 1948/49, from left, Gareth (3 yrs), Basil,
Peter (18 months) and myself.

Part Three

THE FREELANCE PERIOD

THE FREELANCE PERIOD

⚜

Eight

The Mabinogion

I FIRST discovered the stories of the Mabinogion when I was living in Aberystwyth. I found the Everyman edition of Lady Charlotte Guest's translation on the shelves of Basil's study, among all the educational and religious tomes. It must have been part of his library since his schooldays. It hooked me from the start. I had grown up with the Greek gods and goddesses in classical legends, with the wonderful Scandinavian stories of Odin and Thor and Loki, and with the Indian epics of Rama and Krishna. I knew all the tales of chivalry told by Malory, and all the Irish myths. I had fallen deeply in love with one intrepid hero after another, from Achilles to Arthur, Perseus to Parsival. The Welsh tales were a whole new world and I absorbed them avidly.

They are every bit as colourful and illustratable as all the other myths and legends. It is a world of furs, of flame-coloured silk, of torch-light and candle-light glinting on jewellery and armour, of stone fortresses and green forests, of magic and metamorphosis. Yet, the people in these stories are in some way more realistic and human than in most other traditional tales. There are no truly romantic heroes. Pryderi may be the intended hero of the 'Four Branches', as the first four pieces are called, but he plays a minor part. Lleu Llaw Gyffes is completely overshadowed by his uncle, Gwydion, who is older and more of a magician than a heroic warrior. Culhwch is a callow boy, having his first haircut, and seeking help from his powerful kinsman, Arthur. These characters are like men and women of today, even if they once had the status of gods.

Places, too, are real and can be looked up on a map of Wales. There are no made-up names, like Camelot or Lyonesse; we are at Harlech, or on Pumlumon. So the stories are an enchanting mixture of history, romance and parable. Like all the myths and legends which have so intrigued me since childhood, these tales are to be read on more than one level and like all the rest, they present the pivotal moments of time and nature and human experience in pictures. Blodeuwedd is the goddess of Midsummer, created out of flowers which all blossom in June. But, like summer, she is fickle and will not stay in her place, so she is turned into the white owl which haunts our winter nights. In that portrayal of the year's cycle is a whole series of bright, contrasting pictures. I loved the Welsh stories and immediately wanted to illustrate them. To be paid for doing so was a bonus!

When starting on an illustration, my first task is to mark out the space which I have to fill. In filling it I have three aims: to represent a particular part of the text, telling the story in picture form; to reinforce the atmosphere of the whole book—romantic, humorous or mystic; and finally, to make a composition which is pleasing to the eye. This is the most arduous part of the whole procedure, and if I can produce a drawing which satisfies me, the rest usually follows without difficulty.

It is all a matter of balance. The artist balances vertical lines with horizontal, close-up objects or figures, against a distant background, dark against light, strong colour against weak, and realism against imaginative fancy. That does not usually mean a fifty-fifty arrangement; it works better if there is much of one element balanced by only a little of its opposite. The eye and the mind are choosy, and the balance delicate.

I especially enjoy mixing the natural, realistic world with the fantastical. Magic moments such as Lleu's metamorphosis into an eagle, or Gwydion creating hounds out of air, are an intriguing challenge; and they are enhanced if I include objects from the real world, which emphasize the magic by their contrasting normality. I often used sketches which I had made on previous occasions when drawing out-of-doors. For instance, in *Y Mabinogi*, there is a picture of Manawydan catching a salmon called 'A Land Rich in Fish'. That landscape is largely from a drawing done one day not far from our home in Capel Bangor. The distant hills were not in the original drawing, but the water is just as I saw it, though it was a smaller stream than I have made it appear here. Old sketches of plants especially came in useful from time to time. I have to keep quite an extensive reference library beside me too. Birds and animals that I only rarely meet, if ever, have to be looked up and reproduced accurately. I found a series of 'Ladybird' books left by the children especially helpful, particularly four of the seasons, with illustrations by C. F. Tunnycliffe.

When I have a drawing which satisfies me I stretch a piece of water-colour paper, as described earlier, and trace the outline onto it. Then all is ready for the part of the exercise which I enjoy most, the painting.

When I received a copy of Gwyn Thomas's script, it was, of course, in Welsh, but I had the Charlotte Guest translation and knew the stories. Nevertheless, I must read and study the Welsh text that I had to illustrate. I had been to Welsh evening classes for two winters, and had been reading Welsh children's books from the local library, so I could cope with a lexicon beside me to help with difficult words. As it was when I learnt French and Latin in school,

I found the written language much easier than the spoken. I learn with my eyes more easily than with my ears. The mutations slowed me down, but I came through the task and felt more 'into' the text in consequence. So it has been with almost all the books I have illustrated since that first all-important one.

An artist must follow the script carefully. It is all too easy to create a picture which has got fixed in one's head, only to find that it contradicts something expressed in the wording of the text. I was guilty of such an error on at least one occasion. In the story of Branwen, I have drawn the giant, Brân, stretched across the river, so that his followers may use him as a bridge. The text says that they laid hurdles along his back and walked on these; I did not read carefully enough, and have omitted the hurdles. Mea culpa! The error did not go unnoticed by at least one critic. Alas! It is too late now to alter my illustration.

But if an illustrator must be careful never to contradict the script, he may add to it, and often cannot help but do so. A writer could not describe every article of clothing worn by his characters, or every aspect of the scenery, but the artist cannot avoid being confronted with such details. The figures must be clothed and he must imagine the garments; the room or the scenery cannot be ignored. I enjoyed putting my own ideas onto the paper, and even found an author's descriptions hampering at times. I wanted, perhaps, to keep my colour-scheme for a picture to greens and gold, but could not ignore the text which said the character wore a blue tunic, or something equally awkward and unsuitable. "Why can't these authors leave such matters to the artist?" I fumed to myself unreasonably! There was always a way of getting round it if I tried hard enough, so that everyone could be satisfied.

I was told that I could produce sixteen full-page pictures in colour, and I was sent a copy of the Welsh text printed on the proposed size of page in the font chosen. It was up to me to arrange the script and fill in the gaps that were left with black and white illustrations. I always prefer to make my pictures about twice the measurements which they will have in print. It enables me to put more detail into them, and I love detail.

The committee kept a close watch on me, understandably. I was still an unknown quantity, and they were taking a gamble on me! The Art Advisor for the Arts Council of Wales, Peter Jones, vetted all my work and made suggestions occasionally. I attended several meetings in Cardiff, taking with me what I had produced so far.

I had been brought up on the illustrations of Arthur Rackham, and such outstanding artists of the Twenties and Thirties, and I liked very muted colours of the tones that they used. Grey-greens and browns seemed to me the only colours suitable for illustrating myth and mystery, and I abhorred the bright primary colours which were all the rage. These stories were not intended for very small children, but for those who could enjoy tales of magic and olden times. I have always favoured tertiary colours, mixing my pigments into greys and browns, in warm and cold tints; only very rarely using them straight from the tube, and then sparingly. At that time I used three tubes, Prussian blue, yellow ochre and vermilion. With those I could create any subtle green or brown that I wished, and even a perfect black, occasionally putting in a splash of bright vermilion, which I love.

"More colour please!" demanded the committee members. "It's too muted. You must be brighter with your palette!"

I could not bring myself to change! I wonder whether Picasso had his 'blue' period out of choice, or because he was constrained and could do no other? It was as if I was bound and completely unable to splash bright hues onto the page. The Muse simply would not allow it!

"Arthur Rackham would never have had this trouble!" I grumbled rebelliously to a bewildered committee. In the end I suggested to them that I might paint four full-page designs as title pages, one to each of the Four Branches, in the form of illuminated capital letters. They agreed, and I had no difficulty at all in painting these in bright colours. They were not illustrations of the narrative, but echoes of ancient manuscript designs in brilliant colour, and that made a world of difference to my approach. I found the ban was lifted in these cases, and I freely used my tubes, introducing others like ultramarine blue, lemon yellow and alizarin crimson. It even emphasized the grey-green mysticism of the true illustrations by way of contrast.

I finished all the illustrations for *Y Mabinogi*, colour and black-and-white, by mid-July 1982. But you must not think that everything progressed swiftly and smoothly after I had sent in my artwork. The day of publication was more than two years later. The book was now in the hands of the publishers and promoters, and they took text and illustrations to the big book fairs in Frankfurt and Bologna, trying to rouse interest from publishers abroad. There was much indecision about the cover design, and I was engaged to produce at least one which, in the end, was rejected in favour of using illustrations from the book. As late as January 1984 I was asked to produce another black-and-white picture for a frontispiece, which they rightly decided was needed to complete the whole.

I chose to illustrate an incident in the first of the four 'branches', where Teyrnon goes to his stables at night and finds a monster about to steal his colt and leave a boy-child in its place.

For my December birthday in 1982, someone gave me a diary, and I have kept an almost daily record of my life here ever since. So for these years I can turn to it to revive or confirm all that was happening. Here is the relevant entry.

Wednesday, 11th January 1984
"I have got on well with drawing this frontispiece. At the beginning of the week I struggled like mad to get some acceptable picture of Teyrnon cutting off the monster's arm. But I want to include the monster itself and the baby too; and since they are outside the building and Teyrnon with the colt inside, it couldn't be done on conventional lines. Even looking

through the window from outside didn't work because the monster's arm filled the space. So I have abandoned realism, and hit on pure design, with the monster and baby forming a border round the centre picture, which shows the indoor scene. The great arm comes through the window to seize the colt. I really think it works and a ruse like that suits such a book and such a magic subject. It took some working out, though it seems the obvious solution now."

The book was published in 1984 by the University of Wales Press in Welsh, and by Victor Gollancz Ltd. in English. Kevin Crossley-Holland collaborated with Gwyn Thomas in producing the English version, based on Gwyn's translation. There was an American edition, and it was also produced in Danish and Scots Gaelic. It was launched at the Eisteddfod that year, and Gwyn and I were both present. It has been a real success story, and it fulfilled a need for such a publication, to introduce the children and adults of Wales to this great treasure of their heritage. I am proud to have had a part in its creation.

It was entered for the 'Mother Goose Award' (1985) which gives a prestigious prize each year to a first-time illustrator. I did not win that prize, but I was given a generous special mention that I cherish. I make no apologies for quoting it here:

> "Margaret Jones's forceful and detailed work in *Y Mabinogi* (U.W.P.) was much admired; her draughtsmanship is breathtaking in places. There is a real feeling for Celtic decoration here, backed by detailed research, and fused with her own free and inventive imagery. She makes a powerful contribution to a long and demanding text, and deserves a special mention."

I was ever conscious of my lack of qualifications. When people asked, as they did, "Where did you do your training?" I had to admit that I had none. Comments by critics like this were my diplomas and certificates; they were many and all wonderful ego-boosters, with epithets like 'splendid', 'magical', and 'imaginative'—all except one, which arrived through the letter-box to give me a salutary shock. It was a review from the Times Literary Supplement and it called my illustrations in *Tales from the Mabinogion*, "crude and insensitive." "Blodeuwedd, 'the fairest and most beautiful maiden that anyone had ever seen', is represented as a raddled, shapeless, blotchy harridan . . . One must hope that the publishers will at some stage supply the excellent text with illustrations and a format better suited to its severe attractions". Phew!

These stories are among the most treasured in Welsh literature. Most Welsh readers will have known them from childhood, and formed their own pictures of scenes and characters, pictures which I could shatter or damage by imposing my own. As I touch the paper with my pencil I can hear their voices warning me, in the words of the poet, Yeats,

"Tread softly, because you tread on my dreams".

Another critic of the book, Roland Mathias, writing in 'Dragon's Tale', admitted that he had approached it with reservations. He said:

"When I was a boy . . . I disliked stories that were illustrated. So often the pictures cut right across my imaginings. I can hear myself muttering: 'It was not like that at all'. Nowadays, very few children can possibly grow up unaccustomed to having their visual imagination of what they read affected by —often provided by—outside agencies."

Thankfully, however, Mr Mathias had only praise for the 'Mabinogion' pictures, and called the book "one of the most beautifully illustrated I have seen for a long time".

When I painted Blodeuwedd, I was keen to illustrate what was happening, and perhaps more interested in her fickle nature than her beauty. The blotchiness that so offended my first adverse critic is due to the fact that I painted yellow petals on her skin, in parts, to indicate that she was being created out of broom flowers and her hair was made up of oak blossoms. I would hate to know that I had trodden on someone's dreams, and I am awed to think that I may have helped to form those of others; but I can only produce pictures according to my own dreams.

I was approached by the Welsh National Centre for Children's Literature, as it was known then, which has its headquarters in Aberystwyth, with a request to buy all the original illustrations for *Y Mabinogi*. A publisher does not usually buy the artwork, only the right to print it and the originals are afterwards returned to the illustrator, to sell elsewhere if he/she wishes. I have the rights over further printings. On this occasion I was delighted that the whole set of pictures was finding a good home.

They had all the large paintings framed, and allowed them to form a travelling exhibition. The twenty-four pictures were shown all over Wales, and at four venues in Scotland and one on Merseyside. They are currently housed in the National Library of Wales in Aberystwyth.

To my enormous delight I was asked by the Arts Council Committee to produce a design for a 'Mabinogion' map to be sold as a poster, a map of Wales showing incidents from the stories at the sites where they were said to have occurred. This was just, as they say, 'up my street', and I really enjoyed myself. I later on entered the original map in an exhibition of illustrations in the Aberystwyth Arts Centre, and it was bought by the National Library of Wales where it now resides. The poster has proved very popular over the years, and was reprinted by Y Lolfa in 2006.

Since I first entered the world of publishing, my work has been used in a variety of ways and for a number of different products. It has been printed on china—plates and mugs—as a calendar and greetings cards, as table-mats and paper-weights, as a jig-saw, and on boxes containing Welsh fudge. The most bizarre representation

I have not seen, but only heard about. A few years ago, I was visited by an S4C television crew who spotted the Mabinogion poster-map on my wall. They told me that they had recently been to see a master tattooist, who had just completed a major work—the tattooing of my design on the back of a client. Apparently the task had taken twelve years to complete. I gasped to think of the dedication of such a man, the time, expense, and presumably suffering which he underwent, all for a treasured possession that he himself will never be able to see! It must have been undertaken simply to give pleasure to others, and is an amazing piece of altruism. If he ever reads this script and is in the Aberystwyth area, I would dearly love to meet him!

All the time I was producing the illustrations for *Y Mabinogi*, we were in the process of moving house. We had lived on the Buarth hill in Aberystwyth for more than twenty years, and all but the youngest of our brood had now left home. He too would soon be following his brothers into college and employment; and Basil, while I was embarking on a new career, was coming to the end of his. We wanted a smaller house with only one flight of stairs instead of two, and preferably further into the countryside.

In 1979, we went to an auction and bid for a house in the village of Capel Bangor, five miles out of Aberystwyth on the eastbound road. We came out of the auction-room dazed and dizzy, having been successful in the purchase of 'Bronllys', a three-bedroom semi, with a largish garden on the edge of a field.

After some months, during which we sold the old house and painted up the new one, we moved in. I was doing my work in the smallest of the bedrooms and was very cramped and confined. One day Bas said, "We could have a studio built for you on top of the garage". What a fantastic idea! I fetched a ladder and put it up against the wall of the almost flat-roofed garage, and climbed up. Turning towards the north and looking out over the garden to the hill-field beyond, I decided that this was where I would have a big north-facing window, and to my right there would be a door at the top of a flight of steps from the garden. To my left would be an entrance into the house through our bedroom.

So it was, and I sit here now at my board, looking out over the back lawn to a field that rises to a clump of pine trees and in which horses have recently produced three beautiful foals. In this room, on the wall behind me, I painted a mural using acrylic paints on the vinyl-silk surface. It is a fantasy landscape of fields and a castle, a rock-giant, and a cloud-puffing dragon, a dolmen on the hilltop, and a procession of lords and ladies riding past. This is my sanctum, and all the work I have done since was created here. I would rather be here than anywhere else in the world.

While my new studio was being built, I was getting together and framing enough pictures for an exhibition in the gallery of the University of Wales, Swansea, which I had been asked to stage. A van came to collect them all, and Basil, Mark and I travelled to South Wales to see it. I only sold one work, as far as I remember, but comments were favourable. I do not think I would have been happy relying on sales and exhibitions for my artwork. If I had done as my art teacher Miss B wanted me to do, and gone to the Slade School of Art in London for proper training, then most likely that would have been my life. When I visit a big art gallery and look at the works of real masters, it gives me both pleasure and dissatis-faction. I cannot help wondering if I might not have produced works worthy of such a home had I taken up art and learned the techniques of oil or mural painting in a London academy. But it is easy—and pointless—to play the game of "What if?" Had that been my course, I would never have met Basil, or now had my family around me. No, I think I would probably have sunk without trace in water too deep for me; I am doing the kind of art for which I am best fitted; illustration suits me perfectly. I am part of a team and I contribute to a product—a book—that is not only useful but also which can be a greater piece of art than many of those now hanging on the walls of galleries. Providence has made better choices for me than I could, or would have made for myself; and I am content.

In my studio at 'Bronllys', Capel Bangor, Aberystwyth. Behind on the wall is a mural of a fantasy scene that I painted in 1985.

Photograph of myself superimposed on a drawing of the view from my studio at Bronllys. First published in an article entitled 'About the Author', in *Cricket* magazine, Carus Publishing, USA, 1998.

With Professor Gwyn Thomas at the launch of the book, *Y Mabinogi*,
at the 1984 Eisteddfod in Lampeter, Ceredigion.

Nine

Illustration

AFTER I had sent in my artwork for *Y Mabinogi,* I felt flat and
purposeless, an experience which has been repeated in every
similar situation since then. There was already talk among
the Arts Council of Wales members, of another possible publication
to follow—the story of 'Culhwch ac Olwen' from the Mabinogion
series; but they would not embark on that for a couple of years, and
I did not know if I would be asked to contribute to it. Meanwhile,
I had an invitation to produce pictures for a solo exhibition in the
excellent Ceredigion Museum in Aberystwyth. So I had an obliga-
tion to fulfil, a set of pictures to produce; but that is not as firm and
supportive as a commission to make pictures for a set text with
certain restrictions. I had to choose my own subjects and rely on my
own vision and stimulation, and that left me open to self-doubt and
diffidence, an artist's biggest handicap.

Perhaps it is because of my enthusiasm for narrative and illustration that I like to choose subjects in a series. Rarely do I feel inspired by one isolated theme, but a string of related pictures forms more easily in my fancy. I like the stories such a series tells, and the contrasts between one related subject and the rest. So when I have planned pictures for myself, they have been the 'Twelve Months', the 'High Days of the Celtic Year', the 'Planets', or the 'Trees and their Legends'. Now I set out to make four pictures of the Seasons, represented as allegorical figures, to be the main features of the Museum exhibition.

I have always loved the European Spring, Summer, Autumn and Winter, and I missed them more than any other aspect of life when we were living in the all-dry, all-wet climate of India. It seems to me that men and women are at their most comfortable and creative when their lives flow with the seasons of the year. I have always enjoyed making pictures of plants, and including them in larger, more complicated paintings. Painting leaves and flowers is a therapeutic occupation; you have your model in front of you and it does not move. But I would not have been content to be solely a painter of botanical specimens. I included many such in 'The Seasons', making wide borders of them from samples picked around our house, in their proper time. So I could only produce my pictures in season, and each one was done as its time came and went, plucking flowers and leaves during walks down the lane opposite our home.

It was January 1983, and I started off with 'Winter' ('Y Gaeaf'), but could not decide what kind of a figure she should be, and produced one drawing after another, strewing rejected efforts about the floor like a lover writing his first billet-doux. An entry for the diary, 29th January, reads:

> "I lay in bed last night, thinking about how I should like to have made 'Winter' in my picture into a soothsayer, fortune-teller woman, looking into her crystal ball to see the past, failing year, and the future one. At the moment she is too soft and sentimental—characterless. So when they (family visitors)

had departed this morning, I got down to it and have altered
her so that she has a crystal ball and a kerchief round her
head, and red berry earrings which add a touch of colour.
That one point had been bugging me at the back of my mind,
but now I am satisfied."

I don't remember what I meant by "altered her". Water-colour
paints are transparent, and it is difficult to make changes in a picture
without the whole thing looking messy and interfered with. Usually,
if there is something not right, however small, I must start again
from the beginning and redraw and repaint the whole. I have done
that many a time, even with large pictures, and I know that 'Winter'
which was finally framed for exhibition, was the result of a third or
fourth attempt. None of these pictures came easily. Sometimes, if
the work did seem to be flowing effortlessly, I thought there must
be something wrong, and worried about that!

I finished 'Winter' ('Y Gaeaf'), and in early February found there
were some spring flowers already out, so I plunged straight into the
new theme.

Diary, Saturday, 5th February
"A lovely day in the studio, listening to Mozart and Elgar, and
drawing and drawing. I went out first, dug up some primroses
and daisies from the garden and drew them; I then did more
on the main picture. I have altered the tree-girls and I think
they are coming right, but it is a long tailoring process. I have
some good ideas for 'Yr Haf', too, but they are coming too
fast, and I have to put them to the back of my mind, afraid
they will divert my attention from the task in hand."

I represented 'Spring' ('Y Gwanwyn') as a young boy playing
pipes, stretched naked across the sky above a burgeoning landscape.

Diary, Tuesday, 8th February
"Bas came up to the studio about 2 o'clock to ask if I wanted

to go for a walk, but I was unwilling to leave the board while it was still so light (occasional snow showers but a lovely sunny, cold and bright afternoon). He looked at my picture and liked the primroses, of course, but said: "Do you really have to have that fellow there, sitting in the sky? He looks very odd!". I replied: "But he's what it's all about! He is Spring, piping in the season of rebirth". Bas likes plain scenery and nature, but doesn't understand the 'fanciful stuff'."

This memory makes me smile now. Bas had far less inhibitions than I about wandering round our private space 'in the buff'; my all-girl-boarding-school upbringing had left me coy. But, whereas I could freely depict nude figures of either sex, they seemed to worry him—or would he, I wondered, have been happy if the artist had been someone else? I never did find out.

I have never been to a life-class, and I would not know how to go about engaging the services of a nude model, so my knowledge of human anatomy, come to think of it, is almost entirely from pictures. Our modern world is so inundated with representations of one sort or another that it is sometimes difficult to distinguish between first and second-hand experience. I drew the nude figure with the confidence of pseudo-familiarity.

I finished 'Spring' ('Y Gwanwyn'), and longed to start on 'Summer' ('Yr Haf'), but it was only March and no sign of her outside for some months to come. Here is another diary entry.

March 1st
"St. David's Day. What a staunch Welshwoman I am become! I had a long day painting in the studio, and 'Y Gwanwyn' is nearly finished. When I am away from the board I keep thinking, 'It's a mess! I've overdone it. It looks laboured and 'so-and-so' isn't right'. But when I go back to look I find it seems O.K. Which is as well! I'm sure I'd never have the stamina to repaint one so full and detailed on the doubtful chance that it might be better next time! The hyacinth is out

and the scent greets me as I open the studio door. We went for our usual walk this evening and saw our friend the barn owl again—this time along the Melindwr. He is always alone, and seems to own the valley at dusk."

Diary, Wednesday, 2nd March
"Woke early this morning with a bad migraine, but took a pill and it gradually wore off. I had finished 'Spring' completely by 3 o'clock. I'm pleased with it and itching to have a go at 'Summer', but will have to wait about 3 months! Perhaps I'll design the centre picture before then, and put in flower borders later."

I painted 'Summer' as a pregnant woman, and 'Autumn' ('Yr Hydref') as a dual figure, to represent the fruitful and the dying aspects of the year. It was finished before the end of August, using studies of flowers and fungi that I had sketched in previous years. The four pictures were exhibited that September in the Ceredigion Museum gallery, and were bought by the Aberystwyth Council, to be hung in the Town Hall, until a few years later the new County building was erected in Aberaeron, and they have been there ever since. They were printed and are still sold in the Museum as post-cards, as larger prints, and as designs on tablemats.

Encouraged by this success, and still having no binding commitments for another book, I began on a similar set of paintings, in the same style, depicting the months, also as allegorical figures. These too were more-or-less painted in season; as the countryside progressed through its yearly cycle, I scoured the fields and hedgerows for botanical models.

I still agonized over each picture, and the first three, September, October and December, were all painted, rejected and repainted a number of times.

Diary, 7th January 1986
"I painted all day, but am still worried about this one. It is too

complicated and fussy. I must fight the tendency to pour items into pictures wherever there is an empty space."

At times my whole 'career' hung before me, without shape or certainty.

Diary, 14th March
"Repainting 'September' is going fairly well, though I don't feel very bright—so tired and everything such a drag and difficult. I wish I were a true, dedicated, gifted artist, but I don't think really that I should ever have been more than a moderately good illustrator of children's books, and now I would settle for that—if I could be truly sure of it! One book to my credit, and a number of good reviews, seem to mean very little. I want to build on it, but at sixty-six I haven't much time!"

But I wasn't quite so depressed all the time; it wasn't in my nature to lose self-confidence for very long. Sometimes the work developed almost by itself, as if by magic; and then I felt on top of the world.

Diary, 13th April
"I have finished 'April', and am really pleased with it. So rarely, nowadays, do I have one that I want to keep looking at simply to gloat, rather than to reassure myself, repeatedly, that it isn't too bad. I think the last time was with 'Summer', eighteen months ago. I've now decided that I'll have another go at 'September'."

I did, but with little success.

Diary, 26th April
"I painted all morning and much of the afternoon, and felt fairly happy with 'September', but when I had done and put it up in front of me, my heart sank! I knew at once that it "wouldn't do!" It was too fruity, over-detailed and over-

coloured. I'll have to do a cooler, leaner version. I felt very discouraged, but had a bath and got changed to go to the Private Viewing at the Arts Centre. There my spirits received a tremendous lift when I was greeted with the news that the Mabinogion map had been almost certainly bought for the National Library. Their man had been round just after it was hung yesterday, and says it is a mere formality for the Committee to endorse the decision. I could not have wished for better!"

In the week that followed, perhaps buoyed up by that news, I painted 'May', aiming to portray the magic of that time of year using Escher-like tricks with birds and the spaces between them. It turned out to be another one to gloat over!

I continued with the 'Months' until March the following year; but I had no idea what to do with my set of twelve paintings, and they lay, taking up space in the studio. However, in 1987, officials at the Arts Centre in Aberystwyth asked me if I could supply artwork for a small exhibition to travel around a number of cultural centres in Wales. When they saw the paintings they decided they would suit the purpose, and could also be produced as a calendar for 1988. The Arts Centre would undertake it, in conjunction with the *Cambrian News* newspaper, which would print the pictures. The result was the largest calendar I have ever seen, two foot by one-foot-four-inches; and it was sold out before all requests could be met. The pictures have been exhibited since, in sites all around Wales, including St Fagans National History Museum, formerly known as the Museum of Welsh Life, near Cardiff, and the R.S.P.B. Centre at Ynys Hir, near Aberystwyth. At about this time I was also asked for designs for eight love-spoon greetings cards, illustrating some of the best-known romances of Welsh history and folk-lore. The Welsh Lovespoon Centre Ltd produced them, and each card bore a carved wooden spoon.

At last, some time in 1987, I received confirmation from the Arts Council of Wales that they were going ahead with a publication of

Culhwch ac Olwen. The University of Wales Press would publish it, Gwyn Thomas would again write the Welsh text, and as before, collaborate with Kevin Crossley-Holland in producing the English version. To my relief and delight I was earmarked for the illustrations. It is the earliest story of King Arthur, a glorious tale with all the virtues of a true traditional narrative, and a delightful sense of humour, which moves it along at an exhilarating pace. I think I was working at my peak at this time, and I would cite the 'Culhwch' illustrations, and the calendar pictures, as my best work. Illustration may be regarded by some as the Cinderella of the art world, but, as I tell myself when designing and executing a picture, "Be careful! This could be reproduced thousands of times, and turn up in many parts of the world". It is a sobering thought.

When I settled down to work on my second book I found everything easier, and did not have to do so much repainting. I was no longer bugged by the colour problem, and went my own way as I pleased. I found the touch of humour in the 'Culhwch' story very much to my liking; it seemed to act like a drop of oil in the machinery, and allowed me to go slightly 'over the top'. I enjoyed, for instance, drawing two of Arthur's strong men being roundly worsted by the Black Witch!

The Arts Council, too, seemed to have decided they could give me the script and leave me to it. I made a frieze across the top of four pages, showing the hunting of the Magic Boar, the Twrch Trwyth, above the text of that part of the story, and ending, on the next page, with a full-page drawing depicting the seizure of the treasures from between the boar's ears. The effectiveness of the publishers' generosity in letting me work thus with the text was not lost on the critics. After the book was published the *Powys Review*, Number 22, wrote:

> "The illustrations are of five kinds: decorative borders, black and white framed illustrations, marginal or border illustrations, which run across the upper parts of two pages in a frieze effect, unframed line drawings of incidental features of the

narrative, and full-page, in one case double-page, colour illustrations. The richness and variety of the illustrations are
stunning, and all the more so for the way they are integrated
with, and comment on, the text."

He analyses my artwork in a way I could never have done for myself.

"The style of the illustrations varies, but in the main they
draw on the roots of Hiberno-Saxon art, which itself was
an uneasy and variable mixture of Celtic abstract patterns,
Germanic zoomorphic designs, and Mediterranean naturalism."

In making the designs for this book and *Y Mabinogi*, I was helped
enormously by the work of the Scottish designer George Bain, who
studied the art of the old Celtic monks in the *Book of Kells*, and the
Lindisfarne Gospels. He simplified and clarified their wonderful
intricate knot patterns, and published them in his book *Celtic Art,
the Methods of Construction* (Constable). I think these patterns are
extraordinarily clever and intriguing, as well as decorative; and I
love the element of humour in the work of the old monks, who,
I should think, can't have had a lot to laugh about in their lives.
There are threads that end in human or animal heads, and limbs
twisted into complicated knots. My own favourite device is the
small head at the top of a page, hands in the margins on either side,
and feet peeping out at the bottom, with all the expanse of the page
between.

With George Bain's help I sometimes used my own form of such
tricks. I enjoy 'teasing' the viewer, and more than once I have drawn
only the feet of the main character at the top of the page, while his
whole figure is shown, upside down, reflected in water beside which
he is standing. The last colour-plate in *Y Mabinogi* shows Lleu Llaw
Gyffes thus. He is seen, moreover, through the hole that he has
pierced in the stone to kill Gronw. I like to imagine readers turning
the book over, to get the whole picture!

My critic goes on to say:

> "Margaret Jones has an excellent sense of the verbal and visual traditions in which she is working, but she develops her work in independent directions, and has made a style of her own."

That last line in the quote particularly pleases me. If an artist does not have a unique 'style', then he/she has nothing to contribute to art. A particular style is like one's own signature; but it cannot be cultivated, it evolves naturally. I have been told on a number of occasions that my style of painting is instantly recognizable. I find that hard to understand, because I draw and paint as I must, in the way that comes naturally to me, and I can do no other. I cannot read anything particular into my own style, or analyse it. It must evolve from early training, the influence of beloved artists who have gone before, and elements in myself, which I express as I can. Moreover, although it is always my intention to use art like a language, to communicate my thoughts and feelings to other people, yet it invariably surprises me when it does do so. Somehow, if I am drawing, the trend of my thoughts and feelings comes through into the picture, and the viewer picks it up.

I remember once, some years before all this, I was sketching outside, sitting on my folding stool with pencil and board, before a scene which was of a pathway entering the darkness of a patch of woodland. Absorbed in the work, I was surprised to find that a small party of children had gathered around me, very interested in what I was doing. We chatted for a little while, and then one small boy, studying my picture said: "It makes me think of *'The Hobbit'*", which was extraordinary really, because my mind had been full of Murkwood as I drew, though I had only drawn what was before me, a woodland path.

Recently I depicted a fairy changeling for the cover of a book. I was not conscious of giving him an otherworldly look, but one lady said to me: "Oh, I can't look at that little creature. He is so spooky, it gives me the creeps!" Pictures are another language, and can be a powerful means of communication.

Culhwch ac Olwen (U.W.P., Welsh) and *The Quest for Olwen* (Lutterworth Press, English) came out in 1988, and were well received. The Essex review of children's literature, Spring 1989, wrote: "This is a truly beautiful book to handle. The text and illustrations are pleasing to the eye even before a reading of the story begins".

At about the time of this publication I had a fall in the road outside our front gate and broke my right hip. When I came out of hospital I was, for a time, moving about with the aid of crutches. One Saturday afternoon I was in the studio, working on my next project, with, as usual, Radio 4 on the air behind me. It was a regular weekly programme called 'Treasure Islands', which reviewed children's books, and the type under discussion that day was myth and legend. Penelope Lively, a well-known author, was in the chair. All of a sudden I heard her say, "Now here is a very glossy book, 'The Quest for Olwen', with, I think, the most marvellous pictures by Margaret Jones". I stood up with a jerk and laid down my pencil. This was a snippet that had to be shared! So, picking up my crutches I stomped awkwardly down the stairs to share it with my husband. He was, of course, where I would expect to find him on a Saturday afternoon, in front of the television set. The rugby was on, and Wales were giving it their all.

"Guess what!" I proclaimed, standing before him in the middle of the room; "What do you think I heard on Radio 4 just now?" There was a grunt, and I told him, emphasizing my triumph with an ill-judged wave of my crutch. It smashed into a rather nice antique china lampshade hanging from the ceiling, and the pieces all came tumbling down around us. "Yes!" yelled Basil, excitedly, punching the air with one hand; but with the other he brushed me aside and his eyes never left the screen. It seemed that Wales had just scored! I know when I am beaten; it was foolish to think I could compete with the Welsh rugby team, and I did not try. I swept up the pieces of china as he sat in his chair, oblivious to all but the action, and went back to my task in the studio. To be fair to my husband, he was a wonderful support in all I did. But we must get our priorities right!

About this time I was also contacted by the publishers of *The Quest for Olwen*, Lutterworth of Cambridge, and they told me that the Children's Book Foundation were arranging an exhibition in London of original artwork from recent books; would I contribute (framed) the illustrations for Olwen? When I asked how many would be required I was told, "Probably all!" It was quite a task, with only about a fortnight's notice. I wrote to Lutterworth asking for financial help in getting them framed. They declined, somewhat dismissively, I felt, and I paid a considerable sum for a local framer to do the job. There were about fifteen altogether.

Mark, who was in college in London at the time, went to see the exhibition that was staged in the National Theatre and the Barbican Library. He told me, "They dominated, Mum. They took up a size-able portion of the whole display. No-one else had more than one or two!" I felt, with some embarrassment, that I had overdone it; but I had only obeyed instructions. Almost all those illustrations have been sold since, to private collectors. Moreover, a couple of years later, when Pennsylvania publishers were looking for a Welsh artist to illustrate a Welsh lullaby for a book called *Sleep Rhymes Around the World*, they got in touch with the Children's Books Foundation, who gave them my name as a suitable artist for the job. So, as often happens, one thing led to another.

I asked the Arts Council Committee if I might produce another poster, to go with the new books, as the Mabinogion map had accompanied *Y Mabinogi*. They agreed, and I painted 'The Wedding of Olwen', a castle scene, with preparations for the feast, and the banquet itself.

Lutterworth, also, had another task for me. They asked if I would draw black and white illustrations for a book of Indian myths by Debjani Chatterjee, *The Elephant-Headed God and Other Hindu Tales*. I enjoyed the different Eastern setting, and am happy producing pen-and-ink pictures. It is the drawing that is the important part of any picture, and though I love using my colours, line drawing has its challenge and its attraction.

Ten

❧

Snakes and Ladders

AGAIN, my narrative may give the impression that commissions poured in, and life was a smooth passage from one success to another; but the diaries tell a very different story. It was a hectic time, and there were failures and dead-ends a-plenty.

When all the artwork for 'Culhwch' had been sent in, and I was 'at a loose end', I cast around for a new project. As in my art, so in my life, I wanted to fill up every empty space; Nature and I both abhorred a vacuum. I embarked on the writing of a little story of my own, for five-to-six-year olds. It was based on my memory of the small girl who came to play with me when I was about five, bringing her doll's pram and announcing that its occupants had all turned into goblins. I called my story 'A Pramful of Goblins', illustrated it with pencil drawings, and submitted it to Lutterworth Press. It seemed to be immediately well-received, and my hopes rose and sang!

Diary, 20th September 1988

"I had sent off the little goblin story to L.Y. of Lutterworth and she rang to say she was "very taken" with it! She would like to publish but needed co-operation from an American market. If her American colleague agreed, then it would go ahead. She would send me some 'block' books and would like me to design the whole layout."

In the months that followed, I painted and drew and designed so that I had practically the whole book ready, when Bas, ever obliging, took me to Cambridge where I met the children's editor at Lutterworth's headquarters. She was very enthusiastic, and I understood that publication was almost certain. Alas, nothing is sure until a contract is signed, and that, in this case, has never happened. Presumably the American colleagues would not come aboard, and months, years went by, with no result. I still have my 'Goblins' lying unwanted, somewhere in the untidiness of the studio.

Similarly I embarked on a rewriting of Ruskin's story, 'The King of the Golden River', giving it a Welsh mountain setting and Welsh names to the characters. I have always loved the story and wanted above all to illustrate it; and I produced a set of colour-pictures. This was also submitted to various Welsh publishers, including the Arts Council, and the praise and encouragement were unstinted. I felt the work was all but accepted when I was visited by the editor of Gomer Press to discuss the arrangements. But, like the 'Goblins', it was eventually returned to me and the voices fell silent.

Another work, which took up a good deal of my time over many weeks, was a large map of C. S. Lewis' fantasy land, 'Narnia', illustrating all the stories in the series. I took the word of my sponsor who came to commission it that he had an arrangement with the B.B.C. and permission to print such a map to sell as a poster. But after it was finished and handed over, he found he had not cleared the way sufficiently to pass all the copyright laws, and could not print. So all my work went for nothing.

At times it did seem as if the snakes far outnumbered the ladders in my 'brilliant career'. They writhed about in front of me, swallowing my dreams and spewing them out on the studio floor; while ladders with firm rungs were hard to come by. Loud was the praise and prompt the promises, but fine words, as the saying goes, butter no parsnips—though I never could understand what parsnips had to do with anything. They were Basil's favourite accompaniment to his Sunday roast, but they were rather too sweet for my taste.

Sometimes, big failures and disappointments were partly redeemed, and turned into fulfilment of a sort. In a freer-than-usual period, I set out to illustrate, for my own pleasure and satisfaction, in black-and-white drawings, some of the poems of Dafydd ap Gwilym. Even with my limited understanding of the Welsh language, with the help of a good English translation, I could appreciate the wonderful alliterative verse, his dexterity with words, and his vivid pictures.

I completed twelve drawings and thought they would make a good calendar, not too expensive to produce in black-and-white. With Basil's help I took them to Gregynog to ask if the press there would consider printing them in such a form. They were, indeed, keen on the idea, and did make a start on the project. But time dragged on and I heard nothing more, until, after more than a year, the originals were returned to me. Sadly, the Gregynog Press was then in dire straits financially, and was having to close down. Since that time it has been revived and is happily working again, but, at the time, it was another bitter disappointment. It was one, however, which was largely allayed two years later, when I submitted the pen-and-ink drawings to the National Library of Wales, who bought them from me and have them in storage among their collections.

Over the years I took on a good number of private commissions. People came asking for pictures designed to be given as wedding or birthday presents, sometimes landscapes, more often illustrations or flower-pictures. One or two were for star-signs, 'Pisces' or 'Gemini', or 'Libra'. I did not like to refuse any order, and even fitted in a set of black-and-white pictures for an English language book for Italians, commissioned by my daughter's employers in an Italian-English college in Milan. When I had completed the last batch of artwork for these, I had to send it to Milan by courier, postage being unreliable. I was, as usual, a novice, and rang the given number with some nervousness. My call was answered by a confident female voice.

"What firm do you represent?" she demanded.

"No-one really", I said hesitantly. "There's just me".

She found this hard to understand, and my lame explanations were evidently unsatisfactory.

"Do you have a fax machine?"

"No", I said, hardly knowing what it was.

"Well, I suppose you have an e-mail address?"

"Er, No".

"Do you", she queried, with the weary patience of one not suffering fools gladly, "have Headed Notepaper?"

"No", I admitted, my voice now reduced to a whisper.

In spite of my shortcomings, the parcel got sent off and somehow reached its destination. I have learned much since, but still feel like a fish out of water in this ultra-modern communications society. Coaxed along by my family I can nowadays manage to send and receive e-mails, but it is yet another strange world in which I flounder, unqualified and amateur.

Nevertheless, in the midst of all the mayhem, some reliable ladders were set before me, and I planted my feet firmly upon them. Towards the end of 1987, I was contacted by Dr Robin Gwyndaf, former Head of Cultural Life and Curator of Folklore, St Fagans National History Museum near Cardiff and the foremost authority today on Welsh folklore. He wanted a picture-map of Wales, like the Mabinogion map, but showing sixty three illustrations of folk stories, on the sites around the country with which they were associated—another most exciting assignment. I started on the project just after Christmas, at the beginning of 1988, and immediately got absorbed in it, carrying on during the period when I broke my hip and was hobbling about on crutches.

The diaries show that I still worried over every inch of it. Any picture is something of a gamble, but this was large—stretched on a board four foot by three, and I had to keep my fingers crossed (metaphorically of course) from January to the end of March.

> *Diary, 8th February 1988*
> "Painting all day and gradually covering the map. I did Anglesey today, and it is going more smoothly. I am really letting myself go on colour, and using bright blues and greens. A lot will depend on the sea, which must be right! I have to tackle it last of all, and it would be heart and morale shattering, if I made a mess of it after finishing the rest! Anyway—deep breath—so far so good."

The finished map was collected on 25th March and printed as a poster with a bilingual book of all the relevant folk-tales, written by Robin (*Chwedlau Gwerin Cymru. Welsh Folk Tales, 1989*). Both poster and book have proved to be a success, and are still on sale after reprinting. It began a long association with Robin and his wife Eleri, which I value highly. During 1989-98, he sent me, on behalf of the Museum, commissions to illustrate, something like a hundred and fifty Welsh folk tales, in colour and black-and-white. I must have made such pictures for just about every traditional story of Wales; Robin catalogued and copied them all in two collections, and they are stored in St. Fagans, to be used as need and opportunity arise, in books, and on the increasingly used Internet.

Thankfully, too, the Arts Council of Wales had not finished with me yet. They were planning a third volume in the same format as *Y Mabinogi* and *Culhwch*, the story of Taliesin, which is part of Lady

Charlotte Guest's collection, but not included in the standard translation by Thomas Jones and Gwyn Jones. The old team was again brought together. Gwyn Thomas prepared the Welsh script, translated it and together with Kevin Crossley-Holland, produced the English version. I was commissioned to produce the illustrations. The University of Wales Press would again publish the Welsh edition, and the English version was in the hands of Gollancz Ltd., although not long after-wards they became merged into Penguin Productions.

When I received Gwyn's script for this one, I had to sit down and have a long think before pitching in. He had treated the old story as an irreverent romp; it was a cartoon-of-a-tale. Every character and situation was a joke—and it worked brilliantly! Most of the plot can't be taken seriously, anyway, and the characters are all extreme, giving full licence to the artist for unrestrained cartoonery.

I decided I must change my style and adapt it to the tone set for the book by the author. I thoroughly enjoyed the challenge, drawing some inspiration from the creators of the 'Spitting Image' puppets, which were popular at that time. I find great satisfaction in capturing the exact expression I want on a character's face. I drew King Maelgwn Gwynedd looking smug, his queen simpering, his son Rhun being sly and seductive, and the pompous bards looking totally bewildered under Taliesin's spell. The whole set of illustrations was based on facial expressions as outrageous as I could make them, and I had fun! But I had my moments of doubt, too, and wondered if an illustrator who was a skilled cartoonist, and could draw quick, clever sketches would not better serve the book. Such cartoon drawing was not my style, nor was it what would be expected of me; I could only adapt so far. I need not have worried it seems.

Chwedl Taliesin (*The Tale of Taliesin*) was published in 1992 to considerable acclaim. *The Times Educational Supplement*, Junior Bookshelf, came out with a review that praised the work as "an impressive and convincing performance". I was especially delighted to read a child's comments, which appeared after Newcastle schoolchildren were asked for their opinions on newly-published books, in the *Journal*, Newcastle-upon-Tyne, July 1992: "The book is humorous and exciting. The pictures are really detailed. I spent almost as much time looking at them as I did reading the story. The book was altogether brilliant!"

It is, after all, the children whom we aim to please, and I believe that in productions made for them, even into mid-teens or beyond, the pictures play a very important part, as great, indeed, as the text. This has been acknowledged by the Welsh Books Council which awarded their most prestigious annual prize, the Tir na n-Óg, for both *Culhwch ac Olwen* and *Chwedl Taliesin*. I was allowed to share the award with Gwyn Thomas on both occasions, and I am fully conscious of the honour it bestows.

There was one branch of myth and legend that I longed to illustrate, literally the Holy Grail of most illustrators of the genre—the story of King Arthur and his Knights. So when the opportunity of fulfilling such a wish was presented to me, I jumped at it. The commission came from the manager of the Welsh Lovespoon Centre Ltd, for whom I had painted Welsh love scenes, and as soon as I could, I started drawing and painting all the key moments of the drama. Over the months I covered the subjects of Arthur's birth at Tintagel, of the Sword in the Stone and Excalibur, the Round Table and the Quest for the Grail, up to Arthur's departure to Avalon. Alas! This ladder was decidedly unsound; the Lovespoon Centre was liquidated, and I was left with a set of cherished paintings that had no firm future.

After some time I mentioned the pictures to Nan Griffiths, Secretary to, and my valued and helpful contact with, the Arts Council of Wales. She told me that they were considering asking Gwyn Thomas to write a book of the King Arthur stories, to be published in the same format as the three that had gone before. They would want illustrations, and the paintings I had already done might well be suitable. There was a long and somewhat anxious period while everything was straightened out, and I retrieved my

artwork to send it in to Cardiff. After more months of waiting I
finally received a new script from Gwyn Thomas—'Y Brenin Arthur'.
Some of my pictures did not quite fit his text, and I would have to
redo them with differences; some were not covered by his story, and
there were other incidents for which I would have to paint new
ones. I have never undertaken a more enjoyable assignment, and in
1994 I sent in a set of sixteen full-page colour illustrations, and half
a dozen or more full-page black-and-white drawings. Time spent in
Camelot, with Merlin and Lancelot and the rest of the Round
Table, was good!

Again the University of Wales Press (UWP) would publish the
book with a Welsh and an English version. This last was to be undertaken by Leon Garfield, well-known author of *Smith* and other
books for young people. But Gollancz were no longer available as
English publishers, and sadly, Mr Garfield died before he could get
started on a translation. After that, the whole grand project seemed
to drift, and though I rang for information, time and again over the
years, nothing happened. Eventually, the UWP abandoned the idea,
and returned script and illustrations to the Welsh Books Council.

But, unlike the Tale of King Arthur and his Knights, this story
had a happy ending. The publishing company, 'Y Lolfa', with its
own excellent printing press, picked up the baton and were prepared
to publish the book. After the return of the illustrations, I went to
see them at their headquarters in Tal-y-bont, near Aberystwyth. I
had not set eyes on the illustrations for more than ten years, and
found it a strange experience. It was as if they were someone else's
work; I could look at my 'style' and assess it as that of a stranger. I
was not ashamed of them, and I looked forward, at last, before the
end of 2006 to having the book in my hands; that is always an
exciting moment.

For as long as I can remember I have suffered from periodic severe
bouts of migraine, and especially during these years. The diaries
frequently begin a daily account with "Woke with a blinding head-
ache, and had to take pills". Now, at last, in my 'declining years', I

seem to have grown beyond the tendency, and I am thankful for it. In the nineteen-nineties, it blighted many days and slowed me down when I was eager to be getting on with things.

Our children were widely scattered at this point, but we have always remained a close-knit group, and throughout the years they all made frequent visits to our base in Wales. There were comings and goings, marriages and break-ups, triumphs and traumas, births and new settlements, snakes and ladders to be shared. Our small semi was often crammed, and they occupied the caravan installed for them in the garden; my area of work was shrunk to fit the north end of the studio, while camp beds filled the other half. At such times the washing machine hummed daily, and vast quantities of food were produced and eaten. Here are more, typical diary entries, which give a taste of activities that formed a continual background to this narrative.

Wednesday, 15th April 1992
"About 11 p.m. last night, when we were in bed and Bas had dropped off to sleep, Mark rang to say they would be here on Friday for the weekend. Great! So tomorrow must be spent doing their room and getting in stores."

Friday, 17th
"Mark and Claire arrived about 2.30 and I had their room all ready and a ham and salad dinner waiting. They both look well and happy, and they brought a scan photograph of the baby. Everything looks fine."

Saturday, 18th
"I discovered this morning that the cage on the breakfast-room chimney, above the Rayburn, had rotted, and jackdaws were beginning to nest in the opening. So Bas found a new cover and rang Pete to come and help him fix it. Pete came with Ann and the children, and they all had a romping time! Ann gave Mark a saxophone lesson, and Claire likes nothing

better than to play with the kids. I got two big meals and did a wash—theirs as well as ours—and ironed it. I also part-cooked the turkey for tomorrow, and made breadsauce and applesauce, and leek soup, and cleaned all the floors. After tea I went out to admire their work on the chimney, only to discover that B's new 'cage' is my hanging-basket, fixed on upside-down! I had meant to plant that out after the weekend, and had bought some plants to put in it! Ah well! By 9.30 I was knackered, and sank into bed!"

Birthdays, anniversaries and special occasions were always cele-brated with family gatherings. Typical of such joyful meetings was the one arranged for my 80th birthday. We all invaded the Dragon Hotel in Montgomery, Powys, on the few days after Christmas. The hotel management gave us full use of a dining room to ourselves, with a small platform at one end. Our children and their part-ners staged a barely-rehearsed, impromptu 'pantomime' called, 'Pegahontas and the Reverend Basilene'.

Bas and I sat helpless with laughter as Claire took the title role, showing a shapely pair of legs that I would have been proud to own if only! Peter appeared in a large and magnificent feather headdress as Big Chief Sitting Bull, and Chris minced beside him as his squaw, Lying Cow.

The grandchildren took it all much more seriously, and four years old Lewis stormed indignantly onto the stage to retrieve his gun, that was being used as a prop! Our son-in-law, Pino, videotaped it all under very difficult conditions!

The family grew in strength and numbers. They were always our pride and chief concern, and I would never have allowed the Muse to supplant any one of them.

Part Four

TIME FOR
REFLECTION

TIME FOR REFLECTION

✾

11. *Triumph and Loss*

12. *More Beyond*

Eleven

Triumph and Loss

S OMEONE, at some time, somewhere, introduced me to Robert
Graves' book *The White Goddess.* It is about the Celtic Tree
Alphabet, and the myths and philosophies surrounding the
major European trees. There is little that Robert Graves did not
know about the subject of legends, and his extraordinary erudition,
combined with powerful poetic vision, has created a work which I
found compelling. For me it was more of a page-turner than any so-
called thriller, and I absorbed it eagerly, and longed to illustrate it. I
decided to make a series of pictures of the trees and the legends and
qualities attached to them, in between, not with any hope of
publication, which would be very unlikely, but just to please myself.

Accordingly, over a space of about two years, in between fulfilling
genuine commissions of one sort or another, I painted seven, fairly
large water-colours of the main trees. There was the apple, tree of

immortality; hazel, tree of wisdom; willow, yew, oak, holly and bramble. I never attempted to have them published, but in the end presented them to two of my sons, Malcolm and Chris, as birthday presents, and they have them on the walls of their dwellings. Pictures are, in some respects, like my children, and I want to see them comfortably 'settled'; but I sometimes find it hard to part with them.

In the mid-nineties, I experienced a new excitement when I was engaged to contribute in the making of an animation film of the story of Culhwch and Olwen. Louise Jones had set up a company called 'Metta Productions', with sponsorship from the television channel, S4C. She had friends and acquaintances among the Russian animators in the film studios of Moscow, and she gathered a few of them at her home in Llangollen to make an animated version of the Welsh story. I was drawn in as designer for the characters, and drew the figures on which the artist-animator Igor, would base his dramatis personae. Another Russian, Lev Evnovitch, was designing the backgrounds.

It was the time of 'Glasnost' and Gorbachev, and the ice was beginning to thaw in Russian political circles; but things were not easy for them, and they were all finding it hard to make a living, and worried about the families they had left behind. I watched Igor at work and marvelled at his dexterity and draughtsmanship. The Director was Valery Ugarov, married with a young wife back in Moscow. Here is a diary entry:

Thursday, 25th October, 1990

"I met Ira, Valery and Igor, whose artwork is most of the film; he churns out figures and scenes of a high dramatic quality, non-stop. He is to go back to Moscow on Saturday, and is longing to go, having been here since March, leaving wife and thirteen-year old son behind. Valery tells me things are very bad there, and says: "Don't go!" (There was some talk of them taking me back to work for a while in Moscow.)

The streets are never cleaned, and every corner is like a skating rink, with hospitals full of broken-limbed patients! And NO FOOD!' His wife is coming over this weekend, and he will be working in London for a while. He would like to live in this country, and doesn't want to go back. He is very nice, and insisted on showing me a film he has made about Russia. It was a sort of allegory called 'The Cobbler and the Mermaid'. I loved the style, humour and pathos and satire, all mixed up—which is the East-European forte, I think. The Slavic animators capture the magic which some of their American counterparts stamp out with brash cartoon characters."

The film of Culhwch and Olwen which they produced took about half-an-hour to run, when they had completed it, and I loved it. It went on S4C in Welsh, and ITV in English, and will have been shown in cinemas all over Russia. Subsequent films of the Shakespearean stories also involved Russian animators working for S4C, but of course I had nothing to do with those.

One day, in 1996, I received a letter from an American publishing company which produced three or four monthly magazines for children from their headquarters in Peru, Illinois. The art director, Ron McCutcheon, had seen my work in *Tales from the Mabinogion*, and wondered if I would be interested in doing some work for them. He sent a copy or two of their magazine for 8-to-10 year olds, *Cricket*, for me to see. (The title, I saw, was nothing to do with the game, but referred to the insect; there were other magazines called *Ladybug* and *Spider*.) It was a delightful publication, much superior I thought to anything comparable I had seen in the U.K. I lost no time in replying that I would be happy to comply with anything they asked. About a week later the phone rang one evening, and an American voice said, "Hi Margaret". It was Ron, calling from Illinois, asking if I would provide them with illustrations for Rosemary Sutcliffe's *Black Ships before Troy*, a retelling of the Iliad for young people. They were planning on printing it in *Cricket* in nine monthly instalments, and would want three or four pictures for each instalment. My style, said Ron, would suit their publication.

A couple of years previously I had been approached by a London publishing company, Francis Lincoln, concerning illustrations for a story by a Welsh-based writer. He had given them my name as a possible illustrator for his book, and they asked me to take a folio of my work to their offices in the city. They had just published Rosemary Sutcliffe's story, with illustrations by the artist Alan Lee (who also illustrated the 'Mabinogion'), and while waiting to see their art editor, I was looking through it—enviously! The editor, however, did not sound hopeful in regard to my work. She mentioned that they were aiming for an American market, in particular, and said, holding up one of my paintings, "Your style is very—er—English". She managed to make the last word sound derogatory, and I gathered that I would not appeal to the avant-garde American public.

And now here I was, being asked by American publishers, to illustrate *Black Ships before Troy*! "Yes!" I said. "Yes please!" I put the phone down and gave a great whoop of delight. The 'Mabinogion' had been the biggest possible plum, the Tales of Arthur a prize to glory in, and now I was being offered Homer's great epic. There would be all the Greek settings, costumes, armour, ships and pillared buildings; all the action, and the characters, gods and goddesses, men and women; and there would be faces, angry, wily, fearful, expectant, tragic and imperious subjects for my brush and pencil. I couldn't wait to get started.

I was sent the relevant script each month, with spaces for two or three, or more, illustrations. The assignments and the payments arrived smoothly and efficiently; and as instructed, I sent my artwork by the couriers, Federal Express, so that it reached Illinois, sometimes the next day after dispatch. It was all very efficient and I made phone friends across the Atlantic. I was asked to design the cover for one edition, still on the Greek theme, and I painted Achilles receiving old Priam, when he came to beg for the body of his son

Hector. It was shown all that summer at an exhibition of *Cricket* covers, staged in Chicago.

When it was all over, in December 1997, I was unwilling that the link should be broken altogether, so I wrote my own re-telling of the story of Rama and Sita, from the Indian legend, painted illustrations, and sent it to Ron and his colleagues for their consideration. They accepted it for publication in three editions in 1998, under the title of *Rama and the Monkey Host*. Since that time they have printed my retelling of the story of Owain and the Lion, from the 'Mabinogion' collection; and a piece which I wrote about the old Welsh cattle-drovers, each of course with illustrations. They asked me to provide a cover design for the 2001 Christmas edition and illustrations for two short stories subsequently. It has, for me, been a happy and rewarding association.

I was riding high at this time, and one of my most prestigious assignments came from the National Library of Wales, Aberystwyth. Towards the end of 1997, Mike Francis, now Head of Public Programmes for the Library, came to see me. They were planning an exhibition to mark the Millennium, about Owain Glyn Dŵr, because that year, 2000, was the six-hundredth anniversary of his initial rising against English rule. They would like me to design a commemorative plate to be sold in limited numbers, and also another poster-map of Wales, this time showing the history and exploits of the Welsh hero. I readily agreed, but the commission was extended to embrace further work. Ian Cain, the professional designer, whom they called in, asked that I should be responsible for all the artwork. There was almost nothing remaining in the way of historical artefacts associated with Owain Glyn Dŵr; only one item existed in this country. The National Museum in Cardiff had in its keeping a boss from a horse's harness, which bore his shield, quartered in red and yellow, and which had almost certainly been left by him at Harlech, where it was discovered. That, alone, would not make an exhibition, so Ian Cain planned on pictures, blown up to mural size on the screens and walls of the Library ground-floor exhibition area.

I had fifteen pictures to produce of the life of Owain, and immediately set about doing some research and reading books about him. I painted them over a period of about a year, attending meetings at the library each month to show progress so far. It is a wonderfully peaceful and friendly place to work in, and this was a subject very suited to my taste.

The exhibition was launched at a grand opening ceremony early in 2000. All my pictures were enlarged to mural dimensions, and I was pleased to see that modern technology can produce such enlarged copies without losing any of the sharpness or strength of colour of the originals. These had also been contracted down to become illustrations in a book, with poems inspired by the pictures, contributed in Welsh, by the poet Iwan Llwyd, and in English by Gillian Clarke. For the commemorative plate, I had painted Owain as he appears on his seal, mounted with sword raised in his right hand, and wearing a dragon-crested helmet. There was a china mug, too, for which I had painted him enthroned, as on the seal reverse. All these, with the poster-map, were on sale in the library.

The prize exhibit on this occasion was a fifteenth-century letter, which Owain had composed at Pennal and sent to the King of France, Charles IV (nicknamed 'Charles the Mad'). It asked for his assistance against Henry IV of England, and promised, in exchange, to support the appointment of a rival Pope at Avignon, instead of Rome. The letter was still extant, held in Paris, but, on request, the French authorities allowed it to travel to Aberystwyth to be the main attraction in the Millennium exhibition. In recognition of this fact, not only was Mr Rhodri Morgan, First Secretary to the new Welsh Assembly present at the opening, but His Excellency, M. Daniel Bernard, the French Ambassador to Britain, was also welcomed.

I was introduced to them both. Rhodri Morgan looked at me somewhat sternly from his considerable height, as if wondering what I was doing there. He gave his speech trilingually, in English, Welsh, and what sounded to me like perfect French; I doubt if many of our M.P.s could do the same. M. Bernard was charming, and we had quite a chat. He opened the book at the page that showed my illustration of the French fleet arriving at the harbour of Milford Haven, and said, "You have not drawn the French soldiers looking very fierce". I had to admit that they were, indeed, obviously happy and relaxed, but I said, "They have no reason to be fierce; they've just landed among friends".

He used that snippet of conversation in his address to the assembled company a short while later. I was presented with Plate Number 2, the first of 150 having been given on a previous occasion in Pennal, to Alun Michael, when he was head of the Assembly. So the two big stars of this opening ceremony received framed (signed) copies of the Owain Glyn Dŵr poster-map instead. I like to think that one hangs in the Welsh Assembly buildings, and one in the French Embassy—but I doubt it!

While I was chatting with M. Bernard, my grandson and grand-daughter, who had found places in the front row, sidled over, obviously dying to shake hands with him, so I introduced them; though I wasn't too sure about the 'Excellency' title. It is a wonder-ful feeling to know that your grandchildren are proud of you! Basil was there too, but he had been helped to a seat and accompanied by Peter. He was eighty-six, and gripped by cancer. Two operations and a course of chemotherapy had left him outwardly unrecognisable as the man with whom I had run through fire so long ago; but he came and applauded with the rest of the gathering. He was never one to make effusive speeches, and I never expected, or received, a bunch of red roses, or indeed any other flowers; it was not his style. But more than one friend has told me in recent years, "He was very proud of you, you know".

Also present that afternoon was a young man named Guy Pass-more, who had been to see me a few weeks previously with the proposition that he should make a short film about me, hopefully for television. He turned up at the ceremony with his young camera-woman taking photographs, and a week or so later, at our house in Capel Bangor, to make further recordings. I was quite happy for him to do what he proposed, but asked that I myself should figure as little as possible in the shots, and my paintings as often as he could introduce them.

It was the following year when he again came to see me with an HTV recording crew. That television channel had agreed to include a half-hour film about my work, and me in a series called 'High Performance' being screened at that time. The programme went out on a Sunday afternoon, and we made videos of it to send out to the scattered family members.

I am still not comfortable in front of cameras and microphones, and it gets no easier! I feel awkward if the whole thing is rehearsed, and I am trying to sound natural, while repeating a set piece for the third or fourth time. On the other hand, I am not quick-witted enough to cope with an impromptu interview, and I say things which I later wish I had not. I am aware that, in my eighties, I cannot claim to be photogenic, although old age can be an asset, and a useful excuse for a great deal.

During the millennium year, too, I was busy producing illustrations for a book to be published by C.A.A. (Canolfan Astudiaethau Addysg) of the University of Wales in Aberystwyth. It was a collection of folk-tales from seven minority-language areas of Europe: Wales, Frisia, Lusatia, Lapland, Ladinia, the Basque country, and the Romanies. At least two of these I had never even heard of before —the Ladinians from Italy, and the Lusatians from near the East German-Polish border, but the old languages are still spoken among them. The author of the book, *From the Four Corners of Europe* (*O Bedwar Ban Ewrop*) was an Austrian linguist, Dr Wolfgang Greller, who spoke a number of languages, including fluent Welsh. I had to do a good deal of research concerning costumes and background, particularly for the folk tales which were set not only in unfamiliar territory, but also in historical times. There were many differences between the clothes worn in this country and fashions on the Continent in centuries past. However, Wolfgang made contact with the cultural centres in each country, and they sent generous packages of information and photographs.

The book was published at the end of 2000, in each of the minority languages, plus English, but with the exception of Romany. The work involved had brought me much pleasure, new friends, and a widening of my knowledge. It was so important to get every detail right in the illustrations. Every cultural centre was dedicated to preserving the traditions of the people, and I must not violate them. I especially enjoyed meeting a number of visitors from Lapland, who had come to Aberystwyth at the invitation of the C.A.A. They were charming, but had reservations about my picture of them; the reindeer's horns were not true to life, and the pattern on the back of the boy's coat was not authentic. I repainted it, making all the necessary alterations, and when the book was published I sent some of the original paintings to their centre in Kautokeino, Finmark.

In the past five years I have had a happy relationship with another Welsh publisher, 'Y Lolfa', Tal-y-bont. They asked me to illustrate a book entitled *Tales from the Celtic Countries*, written by Rhiannon Ifans who works in the University of Wales Centre for Advanced Welsh and Celtic Studies. She collected and wrote traditional tales from Wales, Scotland, Cornwall, Brittany, Ireland and the Isle of Man. It proved a popular publication, and was awarded the Tir na n-Óg prize for the year 2000. It was also followed in 2000 by a similar volume about Owain Glyn Dŵr for children, and in 2001 by *Saint David*, which also won the Tir na n-Óg award. All these were written by Rhianon Ifans, and published in Welsh and English, with my illustrations, by Y Lolfa press.

All this time Basil's health was growing worse, and he was becoming weaker. As it was when my mother was dying, long before, I could not acknowledge, even to myself, that he was, inevitably, slipping away. I knew, of course, that we were both getting older; but I would say, if we discussed it at all, "Whichever of us goes first", as if that was still a toss-up. It came to the point where he could no longer climb the stairs, or indeed get out of the chair in the front room, and he was admitted to the hospital. We were told that the cancer had reached his liver, and it was only a matter of time before the end came. Even then I hung onto the thought that that time might lengthen to spring, or even beyond. It did not. He was brought home for Christmas, during which all the family came to see him, in the high N.H.S. bed that had been installed in the sitting room, and was called the 'James Bond bed' because of all the gadgets attached. On New Year's Eve, at about two o'clock in the morning, he finally stopped breathing, and we knew that he had gone. More than sixty-one years of love and companionship were over. It is like an amputation of the soul, and I still find myself thinking he is there, as a man who has lost a leg will sometimes imagine he can feel it attached to the body. Living alone without one's constant companion is strange and unnatural. There are times when the house seems about to collapse under its weight of silence. But life, as they always say, goes on, and there was still work for me to do.

2003 saw another publication for Y Lolfa. This time it was the story of Dafydd ap Gwilym, written by Gwyn Thomas, who is an expert on the poet's life, and wrote a wonderfully sensitive account of it for children. I was only too happy to paint the pictures, and this book also won a Tir na n-Óg prize, the fifth time for me, in tandem with an author. Since then Gwyn has written the story of Prince Madog, who was reputed to have sailed to America long before Columbus, and left Welsh influences behind among the Indian tribe of the Mandans. Once again these were exciting and colourful situations for me to illustrate.

At about that time I was asked to illustrate, in black-and-white, a book about Twm Siôn Cati, the legendary Welshman of the sixteenth century, written by Margaret Isaac and published by APECS Press, Caerleon. Life still had much to offer!

I have always, throughout my career, enjoyed meeting and talking with children and young people, and have been invited on a number of occasions to talk in local schools. One year, after the Calendar pictures had been on show in a Welsh town, I was contacted by pupils of the nearby school, who asked for information about myself and my work. It seemed I had a place in their art curriculum.

One young lady asked if she could come for an interview, and she came along to see me in the studio with her mother.

"So", I said, "What are you doing in your art class nowadays?"

"Well", she said, "We are given a list of great artists, and we have to write about two of them, and do work in their style".

"And which two artists have you chosen?" I asked.

"You and Picasso", she replied with perfect earnestness and without the trace of a smile.

I strove to keep my face straight and to answer her soberly. But I thought, Why not? Picasso was a great innovative artist of the like I shall never be; but I do have the edge over him in one important respect—I'm still here!

Twelve

More Beyond

FOR some years, my eyesight has been giving me cause for concern, and a visit to an eye specialist confirmed that my right eye was impaired by macular degeneration, for which there is, as yet, no treatment. I can still see moderately well with the left eye, but must squint, one-sided, at the paper. Drawing and painting have become difficult, and writing is now easier than artwork.

Up to this time, such writing skills as I possessed had been used in the retelling of old tales, such as the story of Rama for *Cricket* magazine. I have always loved word-play, and have at times indulged myself composing humorous, alliterative verses. I am a crossword addict, and cannot do without my daily puzzle. It tickled my fancy, one day, to discover that my name, Margaret Jones, is a perfect anagram of Sergeant Major. When I revealed this intriguing tit-bit to Basil, he said, darkly, "It figures!"

But I had never put together, or written a story of my own telling. At one of our family gatherings, I rashly declared to my grand-children: "Some day I will write a fairy story, and dedicate it to all of you". That is another of the many dreams which, over the years, have come true for me. I had a tale forming in my head for a long time, about a fairy changeling who became a mortal boy. The idea was born out of the many Welsh folk tales that I had illustrated for various commissions, so often that I almost believed in them myself.

Up until a hundred years ago, more or less, most country people firmly believed in the *Tylwyth Teg*, the 'Little People', and I would write a story from their point of view, set in late nineteenth-century mid-Wales. When at last I came to write down my tale, it was already complete in my head, and emerged like Athena, springing full-grown from the head of Zeus. I just wrote it all down without stop-ping, until it was finished and called it 'Nat'.

Basil and I had been able to celebrate our Diamond wedding—sixty years of life together. Among other things we marked the occasion by having a new wooden summerhouse erected at the top of the garden. I look at it now from the studio window, and picture him sitting there, as he loved to do on a sunny day. The family pre-sented us with two gargoyle figures which were dubbed 'Beelzebaz' and 'Pegistopheles', and are the building's guardians. I wrote most of 'Nat' while sitting in that summerhouse, though the black-and-white illustrations had to be done in my usual place, in the studio.

I have not forgotten that Coat-of-Arms, last mentioned three or four sections back. Now I will propose the shield's two supporting beasts. By great good fortune, my lines, as the Psalmist says, have been 'cast in pleasant places', and I am especially grateful that most of my life has been spent in this loved country of Wales. Born of English parentage I married a Welshman, and somehow have become an illustrator of the most treasured literary heritage of the Welsh people, and of the lives of her most celebrated heroes. I have learned to love the mountains and river valleys of this fairest corner of the world, and to value the friendship of its people. The diaries contain frequent passages in which I tried to express my admiration, wishing I had the powers of a poet.

> *Diary, Thursday, 11th January 1996*
> "I was in a bad mood this morning, after a broken night, and outside it was wet and grey, with high winds and the red kite being blown about the sky. But a short while ago I looked out of my window and watched as the dun-coloured hill behind got brighter and brighter, until it was pure gold. The garden in front was dark green in shade, and over the hill a huge, brilliantly-clear rainbow-arch formed against a steel-grey sky. A flock of black and white lapwings tore across the scene. It was magical and I watched spell-bound until it had faded away. A few evenings ago, standing at the front door, I saw a heron fly slowly and ponderously across a new moon. Those are two of the best pictures I have ever seen. I want my eyes to last forever and never grow dim!"

Wales is my beautiful, generous, mother-in-law. Mothers-in-law and dragons have often been linked in the patter of stage comedians, but I will proudly place the Red Dragon in position, to hold up my shield on the left-hand side. On the right I will give the same function to another fabulous beast—the Unicorn—to represent the enchanting world of fantasy, myth and legend in which I have wandered happily all my life. Let him hold in his mouth a pencil and a brush, to show how I paid homage to him as best I could.

For my life, let me sum it up under St. Paul's great triad of 'Faith', 'Love' and 'Hope'. In the department of 'Faith', I might seem to many to have gone sadly downhill during my eighty-plus years. I began life with so many clear advantages: born into a religious household, a strong Methodist family, educated in a Methodist school and trained in a Methodist college. I accepted all that I was taught, and questioned almost nothing. As a child and a young woman, I thought I knew it all and could rebuff any criticism of my faith with confidence. Entrenched in that state I continued until late in life; but there came a point when I wanted to question and argue against the confident assertions made by those who propagated the Christian teaching. They produced such mountains of belief, based on such unproven and questionable premises, that I rebelled. Turning once more to the diaries, I see that my doubts and rebellion keep exploding onto the page:

> *Sunday, 21st October*
> "Went to chapel this morning and squirmed in my seat as S.G. treated us all like a 'Hi-de-Hi' camp or a kindergarten class. B let me blast off about it afterwards, but I don't think he enjoyed it either."

> *Monday, 29th February 1988*
> "The *Guardian* this morning has a piece by a vicar who has resigned from his post because he cannot go along with what he calls 'pixie-dust' which he is expected to dish out to his congregation; yet he wants some kind of faith or belief to hang on to. I go with him all the way!"

Poor Bas bore the brunt of my grumblings; but I sensed that he, too, had queries and reservations about the old familiar tenets. When we were asked to stand and recite the Apostles' Creed during a service, I could not utter more than a few of the words. I kept my mouth tightly shut for all the rest, and was conscious that Bas, standing beside me, was silent too. But at home, he would not be drawn into any argument. I talked too much and too loudly; he found it too hard to open up. One day, long after I had ceased to accompany him to the Sunday morning service, I asked him, "What do you still go for? What do you get from it?"

"The fellowship", he said.

He was right, of course. The church is not defined by the Apostles' Creed, but by the lives and aspirations of its members. During his last year of life I began again to accompany him on Sunday mornings, and now I sit in the pew where he sat, and sense his presence. I had felt that it was unfair for me to reap the benefits of Church fellowship and the social life, if I could not subscribe to the main tenets of the Faith. It would be a kind of cheating, and I had no right to the one without supporting the other. Now I know that what I do have in common with fellow-members is the important part; the rest does not matter. We do not know a lot of what is given out as 'gospel truth', and we do not need to know. I think that Christ, by teaching and example, showed us the important values—compassion, courage and common sense. Follow those, and questions about sex or the virgin birth, resurrection or the after-life, do not need to be answered; they are not important.

So, my bird of faith flew away, and he will not again occupy his old, comfortable perch; but over my shield I will have the dove—hovering.

In the department of 'Love' I have been singularly blessed by many friendships and strong family ties. The name 'Basil' means a King, and in the centre of my shield I will have a crown, as my symbol of him. Around it shall be six stars, with their satellites—our family. Their loved, loving and lovely faces smile at me from wall and mantelpiece, shelf and bedside table. Scattered afar, they nevertheless form the walls of my existence.

'Hope' has ever played a big part in my life. I have always tended to look forward to the future rather than back into the past, not because present or past have been something I wanted to escape from, but simply because life has ever more exciting things in store. There is always a new experience around the corner.

When I was at Trinity Hall, we would stand in our ranks on Speech Day, dressed all in white, like the heavenly host, and belt out the words of the school song, to the rousing tune of 'Men of Harlech'. Each verse ended with a spirited rendition of the school Latin motto, *Plus ultra!* 'More beyond!' I have always loved that motto, 'More beyond' and I will take it for my own, to be written on the ribbon which stretches and curls beneath my 'coat-of-arms'.

Now that 'coat-of-arms' is complete.

PLUS ULTRA . . .!

My 'coat-of-arms'.

The Diamond Wedding Anniversary celebration at the family home, 'Bronllys', Capel Bangor, in 2001.

(Left to right):

Back row: Peter, Gareth, Chris, Mark, Malcolm, Claire.

Middle row (standing): Helen, Seren, Dario, Lara, Tudor, Hannah, Katy.

Middle row (seated): Sue, Ann.

Front row (seated): Pino, Elaine, myself with Josh, Basil, Hilary.

Front (on floor): Sam, Lewis, Lucy, Bethan (Dewi, unseen, born in 2003).

A Selection of Paintings
and Illustrations
from 1952-2006

Typical Mizo houses in Aizawl, Mizoram, 1952.

The Mabinogion. A poster map of Wales commissioned by the
Welsh Arts Council in 1984. Printed by kind permission of the
National Library Wales, Aberystwyth. Reprinted by Y Lolfa in 2006.

An allegory of the month of May from a collection of the twelve months
of the year (1986). Printed by kind permission of APECS Press.

Ceridwen and her son, Morfran, with Taliesin as a baby. First published in
Chwedl Taliesin (Gwyn Thomas; University of Wales Press) and *The Tale of
Taliesin* (Gwyn Thomas and Kevin Crossley-Holland; Victor Gollancz), 1992.

Hanuman setting fire to the city of Lanka in Sri Lanka from the story
of 'Rama and the Monkey Host' (Margaret Jones).
First published in *Cricket* magazine, Carus Publishing, USA, 1998.

Typical Basque scene. First published in the book, *From the Four Corners of Europe (O Bedwar Ban Ewrop)* (Wolfgang Greller; Y Ganolfan Astudiaethau Addysg), 2000.

Design for the Womens' Institute of a banner showing the history
of 1,000 years at Penllwyn, Aberystwyth. Now embroidered, the banner
is hung on the walls of the Village Hall, Capel Bangor.

Early morning matins.
First published in the book, *Stori Dafydd ap Gwilym*
(Gwyn Thomas; Y Lolfa), 2002.

Madog at the Court of Owain Gwynedd, declaring that the world was round.
First published in the book, *Madog* (Gwyn Thomas; Y Lolfa), 2005.

Lancelot meeting a ghostly band of Black Knights at The Enchanted Chapel,
with the enchantress, Morgan le Fay, Arthur's half-sister, in the top
left hand corner. First published in the book, *King Arthur*
(Gwyn Thomas; Y Lolfa), 2006.

Nat, the changeling, at the cottage door. First published in the book,
Nat (Margaret Jones; Gomer Press), 2004.

On a Return Visit
to Mizoram
in 2005

(Photographs by Gareth E. Jones)

A modern-day view of Aizawl and District taken from the Synod Centre.
Strikingly different from 50 years ago, now with electricity, water supply,
cars, television station and computers.

A commemorative stone in Aizawl with the names of Welsh Presbyterian
Ministers who worked in North Mizoram.
(No. 24 shows Basil's contribution from 1942-1953).

With Hmingi, a Mizoram friend, in her house in Aizawl.

With Elaine in Mizo puan dress.

With Elaine and Peter in the Synod Conference Centre, Aizawl,
that was built on the site of what had been the family bungalow.

Appendix

PAINTINGS

1979 'Welsh Landscape and Legend'. Commissioned by the Aberystwyth Arts Centre for exhibition. (Watercolour).

1984 'The Mabinogion'. Commissioned by the Arts Council of Wales for a poster-map of Wales. Held at the National Library of Wales, Aberystwyth. (Watercolour).

1985 'The Seasons'. For exhibition. Held at the Ceredigion County Council Offices, Aberaeron. (Watercolour).

1986 'Months of the Year'. Commissioned by the Aberystwyth Arts Centre and *Cambrian News* for exhibition and calendar (1998). Held at APECS Press Caerleon. (Watercolour).

1988 'Culhwch ac Olwen', 'The Wedding of Olwen'. Poster. (Watercolour).

1988 'Chwedlau Gwerin Cymru', 'Welsh Folk Tales'. Commissioned by St Fagans National History Museum. Poster map of Wales. (Watercolour).

1989 Paintings and drawings of Welsh folk tales. Commissioned by St Fagans National History Museum. (150 completed between 1989-1998). (Watercolour).

1990 Designs for characters in the Story of Culhwch and Olwen. Commissioned by Metta Productions, Llangollen and S4C. A film by Russian animators.

1991 Paintings of Welsh love scenes. Welsh Lovespoon Centre. Greetings cards.

1991 Paintings for poems by Dafydd ap Gwilym. Held at the National Library of Wales. (Pen and Ink drawings).

1997 Paintings of a story from the Iliad, 'Black Ships before Troy'. Commissioned by Cricket Magazine Group, Carus Publishing, USA. (Watercolour).

1998 Paintings for the Indian legend, 'Rama and the Monkey Host'. Commissioned by Cricket Magazine Group, Carus Publishing, USA. (Watercolour).

1999 Paintings for the story, 'The Knight and the Lion'. Commissioned by Cricket Magazine Group, Carus Publishing, USA. (Watercolour).

1999 Paintings of the life of Owain Glyn Dŵr. Commissioned by the National Library of Wales for the Aberystwyth Millennium Exhibition together with a poster-map of Wales and designs for a commemorative plate, mug and trinket box. (Watercolour).

2000 Design for embroidered panel, depicting the history of 1,000 years in Capel Bangor, Aberystwyth. Work executed by members of Penllwyn Women's Institute. Held in the Village Hall, Capel Bangor.

2001 Painting for Cover of Vol. 29, Issue No.4, 'Bringing in the Boar's Head'. Commissioned by Cricket Magazine Group, Carus Publishing, USA. (Watercolour).

2003 'The Drovers'. Commissioned by The Kite Centre, Tregaron. (Watercolour).

2004 'The Drovers of Wales'. Written with illustrations. Commisioned by Cricket Magazine Group, Carus Publishing, USA. Vol. 31, Issue No. 7. (Watercolour).

2005 'The History of Penrhyn-coch'. Commissioned by St John's Church, Penrhyn-coch. (Watercolour).

ILLUSTRATION

1984   *Y Mabinogi.* Gwyn Thomas; University of Wales Press. Also published as, *Tales from the Mabinogion.* Gwyn Thomas & Kevin Crossley-Holland; Gollanz, with Scottish (Gaelic), Danish, and American editions.

1988   *Culhwch ac Olwen.* Gwyn Thomas; University of Wales Press. Also published as *The Quest for Olwen.* Gwyn Thomas & Kevin Crossley-Holland; Lutterworth Press.

1989   *The Elephant-headed God and Other Hindu Tales.* Debjani Chatterjee; Lutterworth Press.

1989   *Chwedlau Gwerin Cymru. Welsh Folk Tales.* Published with a poster-map of Wales. Robin Gwyndaf; National Museum of Wales.

1990   *Tachwedd Tân Gwyllt.* Gweneth Lilly; Gomer Press, Llandysul.

1992   *Chwedl Taliesin.* Gwyn Thomas; University of Wales Press. Also published as *The Tale of Taliesin.* Gwyn Thomas & Kevin Crossley-Holland; Victor Gollancz Ltd.

1994   *Sleep Rhymes around the World.* Jane Yollen; Boyd Mills Press, USA.

1999   *Chwedlau Celtaidd.* Also published in English as *Tales from the Celtic Countries.* Rhiannon Ifans; Y Lolfa, Tal-y-bont.

2000   *Gronw's Stone.* Ann Gray and Edmund Cusick. Headland Press, Liverpool.

2000   *From the Four Corners of Europe (O Bedwar Ban Ewrop).* Wolfgang Greller; Y Ganolfan Astudiaethau Addysg, University of Wales, Aberystwyth (Welsh & English). Also published by co-publishers in The Netherlands, Norway, Germany and Italy.

2000   *Owain Glyn Dŵr 1400-2000.* Iwan Llwyd (Welsh), Gillian Clarke (English); National Library of Wales, Aberystwyth.

2000   *Owain Glyn Dŵr, Tywysog Cymru.* Also published in English as *Owain Glyn Dŵr, Prince of Wales.* Rhiannon Ifans; Y Lolfa, Tal-y-bont.

2001   *Blodeuwedd.* Anthology of Poems; Edmund Cusick; Headland Press, Liverpool.

2002   *Dewi Sant.* Rhiannon Ifans; Y Lolfa, Tal-y-bont. Also an edition in English (*Saint David*).

2002   *Stori Dafydd ap Gwilym.* Gwyn Thomas; Y Lolfa, Tal-y-bont. Also an edition in English (*The Story of Dafydd ap Gwilym*).

2004   *Nat.* Margaret Jones; Gomer Press, Llandysul.

2005   *The Tale of Twm Siôn Cati.* Margaret Isaac; APECS Press Caerleon.

2005   *Madog.* Gwyn Thomas; Y Lolfa, Tal-y-bont.

2006 *Y Brenin Arthur.* Gwyn Thomas; Y Lolfa, Tal-y-bont. Also an edition in English (*King Arthur*).

2006 *Nat and the Box of Gifts.* Margaret Jones; University of Wales Institute, Cardiff.

In the Press:

Llyfr Datguddiad Ioan. The Revelation of John; Margaret Jones. Edited and published by Robin Gwyndaf and printed by Cambrian Press, Aberystwyth.

Llywelyn, ein Llyw Olaf; Gwyn Thomas. Also to be published in English: *Llywelyn, the Last Prince of Wales.* Y Lolfa, Tal-y-bont.

EXHIBITIONS

1960-1970 Joint exhibitions with fellow members of the Cardiganshire Art Society Annual Exhibition (Welsh stories and landscape).

1979 Solo exhibition at the Arts Centre, Aberystwyth (Welsh Landscape and Legend).

1980 Joint exhibition with a fellow artist at the Information Centre, Aberystwyth (Welsh Landscape and Legend).

1982 Solo exhibition of watercolour paintings at the Ceredigion Museum, Aberystwyth.

1983 Solo exhibition of watercolour paintings at University College, Swansea.

1984 Travelling exhibition of the 'Mabinogi' illustrations to various venues in Wales, Merseyside and Scotland, arranged by the Welsh Books Council.

1987 Joint exhibition with other artists at the National Theatre and the Barbican Gallery, London, of recent children's book illustrations (*Culhwch ac Olwen*).

1988 Solo exhibition of 'The Months of the Year' at the Arts Centre, Aberystwyth, followed by a travelling exhibition of 'The Months' to various venues in Wales, including St Fagans National History Museum, the Central Library, Cardigan and the Royal Society for the Protection of Birds Centre, Ynys-hir.

1997 Joint exhibition of covers for *Cricket* magazine, Chicago, USA.

AWARDS

The Welsh Books Council's Tir na n-Óg prize was awarded jointly with the authors for the illustrations of their books.

1988 *Culhwch ac Olwen*. Gwyn Thomas; University of Wales Press.
1992 *Chwedl Taliesin*. Gwyn Thomas; University of Wales Press.
1999 *Chwedlau Celtaidd*. Rhiannon Ifans; Y Lolfa.
2001 *Dewi Sant*. Rhiannon Ifans; Y Lolfa.
2003 *Stori Dafydd ap Gwilym*. Gwyn Thomas; Y Lolfa.

ADDITIONAL INFORMATION

1990 Featured as the subject of an article by the Editor in the periodical, *The New Welsh Review*, Vol. 2, No. 4; 'Margaret Jones; Images for Words'.
Cover designs and use of pictures placed in subsequent issues of *New Welsh Review*; Vol. 7, No. 25; Vol. 11, No. 42, and in *The Powys Review*, Vol. 9, No. 25.
2003 Featured as the subject of a half-hour programme by Harlech Television in a series entitled, *High Performance.*
2004 Featured in the July/August issue in *Cambria* magazine in an article entitled, 'The Fabulous Talent of Margaret Jones'.
2005 Featured as the author and illustrator of the book, *Nat*, in the periodical, *English in Wales* (Summer issue).

1984-2004 Margaret Jones's illustrations have been associated with books in the Welsh and English languages, and with translations of the books into the Gaelic, Danish, Friesian, Basque, Ladinian, Sami and Sorbian languages.